Strategic Management

Dr.M.A. Raajarajeswari

D. Divya

Published by

BONFRING®
Intellectual Integrity

ISBN 978-93-87862-11-1

Authors

Dr.M.A. Raajarajeswari

D. Divya

Bonfring

309, 2nd Floor,

5th Street Extension, Gandhipuram,

Coimbatore-641 012.

Tamilnadu, India.

E-mail: info@bonfring.org

Website: www.bonfring.org

Phone: 0422 4213231

Preface

Strategic Management is a wide and diverse subject. This book is drafted and designed to acquaint the readers with all the concepts and theories relevant to the subject. It will serve as a foundation to prepare for the examination for all the undergraduate and post graduate students of any program having Strategic Management as a part of it. It is a common subject and need of the hour for students of commerce and management stream.

We hope that teachers, students and practicing managers will find this book highly useful. We could be very much obliged to receive suggestions from the readers for improving the standard of the book.

We take this opportunity to offer our sincere thanks to our Principal, Head, Colleagues, family, friends and publisher for bringing out this book in its excellent form.

Dr.M.A. Raajarajeswari

D. Divya

Authors Profile

Dr.M.A. Raajarajeswari, B.Com., MBA., M.Phil., Ph.D., is an Assistant Professor in Management at Hindusthan College of Arts and Science(HICAS), Coimbatore. Prior to HICAS she has served as an Assistant Professor in an Engineering College, a B-School and in corporate. With her industry, teaching and research experience she has written and published in various National and International Journals. She has also presented in many National and International Conferences. She is also a review board member for a reputed international journal. Her objective is to give her insights in the form of books and bridge the gap between academics and industry for the students and management professionals.

D. Divya, B.Com(CS)., MBA., M.Com., M.Phil., PGDCA., PGDED.,(Ph.D)., is an Assistant Professor in Management at Hindusthan College of Arts and Science(HICAS), Coimbatore. She has more than Nine years of teaching experience in Business Administration and Commerce. She has published various articles in referred journals and has presented National and International level Seminars and Conferences. Her areas of interests are Financial Services, Principles of Management, Strategic Management and Marketing Management.

Syllabus

Chapter I

Strategic Management

Strategic Management- Meaning- Definition- Nature- Significance- Elements- Strategic Management Process- Corporate Strategy- Strategic Planning- Nature- Scope- Importance- Process- Decision making- Mission- Vision- Objectives- Goals- Levels of strategy.

Chapter II

External Environment

Environmental Analysis- Porter's Five Forces Model- Environmental Scanning- Situational Analysis- SWOT- TOWS- ETOP- Value chain analysis- Competitive advantage and Core competencies.

Chapter III

Strategic Analysis

Strategic Choice- Process- BCG Matrix- Mc Kinsey's 7S Model- Gap analysis- GE Matrix- Portfolio analysis- Balanced Score Card- Competitor analysis- Life cycle analysis.

Chapter IV

Strategic Formulation and Implementation

Strategic Formulation and Implementation- concept- Steps- Factors- Approaches- Process- Resource allocation- Designing organisational structure- Control system- Matching structure and control- Strategic positioning- Routes to competitive advantage.

Chapter V

Strategic Evaluation and Control

Strategic Evaluation and Control- Importance- Criteria- Qualitative and Quantitative factors- Strategic Control- Types/ Techniques- Process- Factors of effective evaluation and control system.

Chapter VI

Other Strategic Issues

Other Strategic Issues- Managing Technology and innovation- Mergers and acquisition- Diversification- Global issues and challenges in strategic management- Business Process Reengineering- Total Quality management- Benchmarking- Six Sigma- Corporate Social Responsibility- Ethics- Social Audit- Corporate governance.

<table>
<tr><th>Chapter</th><th>Contents</th><th>Page No</th></tr>
</table>

I	**Strategic Management**	**1**
	1. Strategic Management	1
	1.1. Nature of Strategic Management	1
	1.2. Importance of Strategic Management	2
	1.3. Elements of Strategic Management	4
	1.4. The Scope of Strategic Management	5
	1.5. Dimensions of Strategic Management	5
	1.6. Levels of Strategy	7
	1.7. Strategic Planning	9
II	**External Environment**	**20**
	2.1. Environmental Analysis	20
	2.2. Environmental Scanning	20
	2.3. Situational Analysis	21
	2.4. Porter's Five Forces Model	25
	2.5. SWOT Analysis	29
	2.6. SWOT/TOWS Matrix	31
	2.7. Environmental Threat and Opportunity Profile (ETOP)	32
	2.8. Value Chain Analysis (VCA)	33
	2.9. Competitive Advantage	36
III	**Strategic Analysis**	**39**
	3.1. Strategic Choice	39
	3.2. BCG Matrix	39
	3.3. McKinsey 7s Model	41
	3.4. Strategic Gap Analysis	45
	3.5. Balanced Score Card	51
	3.6. Life Cycle Analysis	52

IV	**Strategic Formulation and Implementation**	**54**
	4.1. Strategic Implementation	54
	4.2. Functions of Top Level Management	62
	4.3. Role of the CEO and Management	63
	4.4. Matching Structure Strategy	65
	4.5. Resource Allocation	66
V	**Strategic Evaluation and Control**	**71**
	5.1. Strategic Evaluation and Control	71
	5.2. Importance of Strategic Evaluation and Control	71
	5.3. Evaluation and Control Criteria	72
	5.4. Quantitative and Qualitative Factors	85
	5.5. Strategy Evaluation	87
	5.6. Categories of Evaluation	88
VI	**Other Strategic Issues**	**90**
	6.1. Managing Technology and Innovation	90
	6.2. Mergers and Acquisitions	92
	6.3. Diversification	96
	6.4. Global Issues and Challenges in Strategic Management	98
	6.5. Total Quality Management	99
	6.6. Benchmarking	102
	6.7. Six Sigma	106
	References	**112**
	Question Bank	

CHAPTER I

STRATEGIC MANAGEMENT

Strategy

The word "strategy" is derived from the Greek word "stratçgos"; stratus (meaning army) and "ago" (meaning leading/moving).

Strategy is an action that managers take to attain one or more of the organization's goals. Strategy can also be defined as "A general direction set for the company and its various components to achieve a desired state in the future. Strategy results from the detailed strategic planning process".

1. Strategic Management

Strategic management is the management of an organization's resources to achieve its goals and objectives. Strategic management involves setting objectives, analysing the competitive environment, analysing the internal organization, evaluating strategies and ensuring that management rolls out the strategies across the organization. At its heart, strategic management involves identifying how the organization stacks up compared to its competitors and recognizing opportunities and threats facing an organization, whether they come from within the organization or from competitors.

According to **B. H. Liddell Hart** strategy is "the art of the employment of battles as a means to gain the object of war'.

According to **Kenneth Andrews** "Strategy is the pattern of decisions in a company that determines and reveals its objectives, purposes, or goals, produces the principal policies and plans for achieving those goals, and defines the range of business the company is to pursue, the kind of economic and human organization it is or intends to be, and the nature of the economic and non-economic contribution it intends to make to its shareholders, employees, customers, and communities".

1.1. Nature of Strategic Management

The nature of Strategic Management is different from other aspects of management as it demands attention to the "big picture" and a rational assessment of the future options. It provides:

- a strategic direction endorsed by the team and stakeholders
- a clear business strategy and vision for the future
- a mechanism for accountability
- a framework for governance at the various levels

- a coherent framework for managing risk for ensuring business continuity
- the ability to exploit opportunities and respond to external change by taking ongoing strategic decisions

1.2. Importance of Strategic Management

Due to the strategic management company receives the following type of economic and non- economic importance. They are:

- **Alertness in Employees:** The alertness among the employees increases the success of objectives and targets due to strategic management. While framing the strategy management studies the capability and weakness of employees and resources and taking the steps to improve them, the employees become more alert about their own performance and the group activity.

- **Increase in the Efficiency of the Employees:** The officers and experienced employees of all the three levels of re-engagement are included in strategic management process. The necessary inter-process in being done with them and for the success of strategy necessary training is also given to them. By this there is a notable increase in efficiency of employees and they get inspiration to work more.

- **Increase in Profitability:** The profitability of a unit depends upon-the maximum use of limited resources. Through strategically management process, the managers cannot only make the maximum use of financial resources but also, they can use maximum man power to increase the overall productivity and profitability of the unit.

- **Reduction in Fixed and Flexible Expense:** The capital invested in the fixed assets is a fixed capital. Instead of purchasing the fixed assets, the managers may buy such assets on rent to decrease the fixed capital investment. In the same way, the flexible expenses can also be reduced through collection arrangement. Making changes in packing, of making changes in full, by acceptance, the strategy of machinery resources in management etc.

- **Motivation to Group Activity:** By taking strategic decisions through the group, integration between group members increases on accepting various optional strategies which result in to co-operation and unity. Not only that, but the managers can also get the advantage of special strength of group members.

- **Reduction in cost of capital:** It is a fact that the unit which is successful in raising the capital of the lowest possible cost is almost eligible to face the competition right from the beginning. After getting the estimate of capital requirement, the managers select the sources of capital from where they can acquire the capital in a strategically manner. The strategic management has been proved to be very useful to raise the estimated capital at lowest possible rate, simple conditions for mortgage, return of borrowed capital and conversion of borrowed capital into owner's capital.

- **Acceptance of Organizational Changes:** Normally the employees do not accept the changes made in the organization, because due to that the change occurs in their roles also. As a result, the necessity to giving training of the new work to the employees arises. Not only that but because of such changes many departments also have to be closed. In these circumstances the problem of the safety of job arises. In strategic management process the capability of employees is also considered. Not only that, but for its development, efforts are made through training programmed so no question arises for the employees for not accepting the changes.

- **Increase in rate of return on investment:** Due to the strategic management there is a noble increase in the rate of return on investment made in the project. On the basis of the information received through analysis of internal and external environment the managers can increase the rate of return on investment by making a maximum use of resources.

- **Prevention of Overlapping of Work:** Due to the interaction with employees and officers working at all the levels of the organization the question does not arise at all for the distribution of one work to more than one employee or event he overlapping work is also not possible. When the same activity is done by more than one employee. At that time there is wastage of time and materials. The problem of co-ordination also arises. With the help of strategic process, the managers can prevent the overlapping of work.

- **Prevention of Organizational Gap:** Out of the departmental activities organization if any activity is not allotted to any employee, that activity is known as organizational gap. If the allotment of any work is left out by mistake, then none of the employees can be held responsible for it. In strategic management process, because of the interacting process being done with each employee, all the employees are given equal works and so there does not arise a question of organizational gaps.

- **Increase in trading on equity:** Trading on equity depends upon many factors. Among on this, by making a maximum use of borrowed capital in a creative manner through strategic management process, the profitability of the unit can be increased and the equity share holders can be paid maximum dividend. If an appropriate strategically arrangement is not made for the use of financial resources, then its profitable use will not be successful and the interest on the borrowed capital will also become burdensome.

1.3. Elements of Strategic Management

Strategic management includes goal-setting, planning and evaluation steps. After company leaders establish objectives for the organization, the four strategic management elements used to achieve it include environmental scanning, strategy formulation, strategy implementation, and evaluation and control. These elements helps develop effective business tactics and evaluate performance relative to goals.

Environmental Analysis

Environmental analysis involves comparing the company's situation to opportunities and threats in the external environment. Factors such as the economy, regulations, competition, societal changes, customer preference changes, technological advances and the environmental all could impact the environmental scan. A strengths, weaknesses, opportunities and threats analysis is a standard tool used in this stage. Conducting a SWOT assessment gives leaders a good picture of current internal strengths and weaknesses relative to external business opportunities and potential threats.

Strategy Formulation

In formulating a strategy, leaders want to leverage core strengths and protect against threats to areas of vulnerability. If a business has advanced technology or services, an improving economy presents an opportunity to effectively communicate the importance of value to a discerning target market. In contrast, if economic conditions soften, company leaders must decide whether to continue to promote in the same way or offer discounts to budget-conscious buyers. Retraining service employees to better connect with value-oriented consumers is another approach to building strong, loyal customer relationships.

Strategy Implementation

The implementation element of strategic management involves taking action. Company leaders communicate the strategy to internal leaders who then pass on roles and responsibilities to their team members. Each department and employee may have a modified role in implementing a new strategy, which may require leveraging outside resources. A customer service manager may hire an external service training organization, for example, to implement a strategy to improve service performance in order to strengthen customer relationships.

Evaluation and Control

Successful leaders don't just expect, they inspect. This point contributes to the purpose of the fourth element-evaluation and control. As departments and workers carry out their responsibilities toward goals, supervisors assess performance. A key component of evaluation is quantified goals. The service department could have a 95 percent customer satisfaction objective, for instance. Over time, managers evaluate their workers and attempt to correct deficiencies.

1.4.   The Scope of Strategic Management

Constable has defined the area addressed by strategic management as "the management processes and decisions which determine the long-term structure and activities of the organization". This definition incorporates five key themes:

- Management process. Management process as relate to how strategies are created and changed.
- Management decisions. The decisions must relate clearly to a solution of perceived problems (how to avoid a threat; how to capitalize on an opportunity).
- Time scales. The strategic time horizon is long. However, it for company in real trouble can be very short.
- Structure of the organization. An organization is managed by people within a structure. The decisions which result from the way that managers work together within the structure can result in strategic change.
- Activities of the organization. This is a potentially limitless area of study and we normally shall centre upon all activities which affect the organization.

1.5.   Dimensions of Strategic Management

Strategic management process involves the entire range of decisions. Typically, strategic issues have six identifiable dimensions:

- Strategic issues require top-management decisions
- Strategic issues involve the allocation of large amounts of company resources
- Strategic issues are likely to have significant impact on the long-term prosperity of the firm
- Strategic issues are future oriented
- Strategic issues usually have major multifunctional or multi-users consequences
- Strategic issues necessitate considering factors in the firm's external environment.

Strategic Management Process

Strategic Management Process is a series of steps which are defined as the way an organization defines its strategy along with all the stakeholders. Strategic Management Process is a continuous process in which the organization decides to implement a selected few strategies, details the implementation plan and keeps on appraising the progress & success of implementation through regular assessment.

The strategic management process is a five stage process as shown in the figure below. The process is not a onetime implementation but we can think strategic management process as a loop which keeps on going to achieve the objectives as per the need.

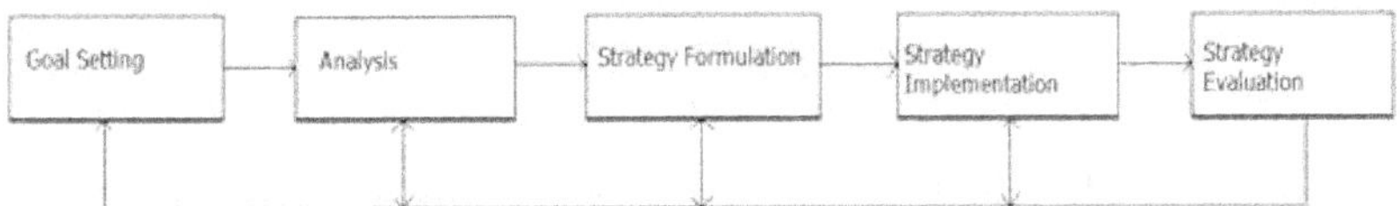

i. *Goal Setting*

The vision and goals of the organization are clearly stated. The short-term and long-term goals are defined, processes to achieve the objectives are identified and current staff is evaluated to choose capable people to work on the processes.

ii. *Analysis*

Data relevant to achieve the goals of the organization is gathered, potential internal and external factors that can affect the sustainable growth of the organization are examined and SWOT analysis is also performed.

iii. *Strategy Formulation*

Once the analysis is done, the organization moves to the Strategy Formulation stage where the plan to acquire the required resources is designed, prioritization of the issues facing the business is done and finally the strategy is formulated accordingly

iv. *Implementation*

After formulation of the strategy, the employees of the organization are clearly made aware of their roles and responsibilities. It is ensured that funds would be available all the time. Then the implementation begins.

v. Strategy Evaluation

In this process, the strategies being implemented are evaluated regularly to check whether they are on track and are providing the desired results. In case of deviations, the corrective actions are taken.As shown in the figure, the five stages are not stand-alone and constantly interact with each other in order to ensure better management of the business.

1.6. Levels of Strategy

Strategy may operate at different levels of an organization – corporate level, business level, and functional level. The strategy changes based on the levels of strategy.

1. **Corporate level strategy:** This level answers the foundational question of what you want to achieve. Is it growth, stability, or retrenchment?
2. **Business unit level strategy:** This level focuses on how you're going to compete. Will it be through customer intimacy, product or service leadership, or lowest total cost? What's the differentiation based on?
3. **Market level strategy:** This strategy level focuses on how you're going to grow. Will it be through market penetration, market development, product or service development, or diversification?

Corporate Level Strategy

Corporate level strategy occupies the highest level of strategic decision making and covers actions dealing with the objective of the firm, acquisition and allocation of resources and coordination of strategies of various SBUs for optimal performance.

Top management of the organization makes such decisions. The nature of strategic decisions tends to be value-oriented, conceptual and less concrete than decisions at the business or functional level.

Business-Level Strategy

Business level strategy is–applicable in those organizations, which have different businesses-and each business is treated as strategic business unit (SBU). The fundamental concept in SBU is to identify the discrete independent product/market segments served by an organization.Since each product/market segment has a distinct environment, a SBU is created for each such segment. For example, Reliance Industries Limited operates in textile fabrics, yarns, fibers, and a variety of petrochemical products. For each product group, the nature of market in terms of customers, competition, and marketing channel differs.

Therefore, it requires different strategies for its different product groups. Thus, where SBU concept is applied, each SBU sets its own strategies to make the best use of its resources (its strategic advantages) given the environment it faces. At such a level, strategy is a comprehensive plan providing objectives for SBUs, allocation of resources among functional areas and coordination between them for making optimal contribution to the achievement of corporate-level objectives.

Such strategies operate within the overall strategies of the organization. The corporate strategy sets the long-term objectives of the firm and the broad constraints and policies within which a SBU operates. The corporate level will help the SBU define its scope of operations and also limit or enhance the SBUs operations by the resources the corporate level assigns to it. There is a difference between corporate-level and business-level strategies.

For example, Andrews says that in an organization of any size or diversity, corporate strategy usually applies to the whole enterprise, while business strategy, less comprehensive, defines the choice of product or service and market of individual business within the firm. In other words, business strategy relates to the 'how' and corporate strategy to the 'what'. Corporate strategy defines the business in which a company will compete preferably in a way that focuses resources to convert distinctive competence into competitive advantage.'

Corporate strategy is not the sum total of business strategies of the corporation, but it deals with different subject matter. While the corporation is concerned with and has impact on business strategy, the former is concerned with the shape and balancing of growth and renewal rather than in market execution.

Functional-Level Strategy

Functional strategy, as is suggested by the title, relates to a single functional operation and the activities involved therein. Decisions at this level within the organization are often described as tactical. Such decisions are guided and constrained by some overall strategic considerations.

Functional strategy deals with relatively restricted plan providing objectives for specific function, allocation of resources among different operations within that functional area and coordination between them for optimal contribution to the achievement of the SBU and corporate-level objectives.

Below the functional-level strategy, there may be operations level strategies as each function may be dividend into several sub functions. For example, marketing strategy, a functional strategy, can be subdivided into promotion, sales, distribution, pricing strategies with each sub function strategy contributing to functional strategy.

Difference between Strategy and Tactics

Basis for Comparison	Tactics	Strategy
Meaning	A carefully planned action made to achieve a specific objective is Tactics.	A long-range blue print of an organization's expected image and destination is known as Strategy.
Concept	Determining how the strategy be executed.	An organized set of activities that can lead the company to differentiation.
Nature	Preventive	Competitive
What is it?	Action	Action plan
Focus on	Task	Purpose
Formulated at	Middle level	Top level
Risk involved	Low	High
Approach	Reactive	Proactive
Flexibility	High	Comparatively less
Orientation	Towards the present conditions	Future oriented

1.7. Strategic Planning

A comprehensive planning process designed to determine how the firm will achieve its mission, goals, and objectives over the next five or ten years or longer.

Nature of Strategic Planning

Strategic planning is an organizational management activity that is used to set priorities, focus energy and resources, strengthen operations, ensure that employees and other stakeholders are working toward common goals, establish agreement around intended outcomes/results, and assess and adjust the organization's direction in response to a changing environment. It is a disciplined effort that produces fundamental decisions and actions that shape and guide what an organization is, who it serves, what it does, and why it does it, with a focus on the future. Effective strategic planning articulates not only where an organization is going, and the actions needed to make progress, but also how it will know if it is successful.

Importance

The benefits of strategic planning at the corporate level include:

- consensus on key issues and strategies to address them
- commitment to, and capacity for, implementing the strategies
- clearer communication of priorities
- improved cooperation among those pursuing strategic objectives, and
- more effective management control of strategic initiatives.

Strategic Planning Process

A Model of the Strategic Planning Process

The formal strategic planning process has five main steps:

1. Selection of corporate mission and major corporate goals.
2. Analysing the organization's external competitive environment to identify opportunitiesand threats.
3. Analysing the organization's internal operating environment to identify the organization'sstrengths and weaknesses.
4. Selecting the strategies that build on the organization's strengths and correct its weaknesses in order to take advantage of external opportunities and counter external threats. These strategies should be consistent with the mission and major goals of the organization. They should be congruent and constitute a viable business model.
5. Formulating and Implementing the strategies. The task of analysing the organization's external and internal environments and then selecting appropriate strategies constitutes strategy formulation. In contrast, as noted earlier, strategy implementation involves putting the strategies (or plan) into action. This includes taking actions consistent with the selected strategies of the company at the corporate, business, and functional levels; allocating roles and responsibilities among managers (typically through the design of organizational structure); allocating resources (including capital and money); setting short-term objectives; and designing the organization's control and reward systems.

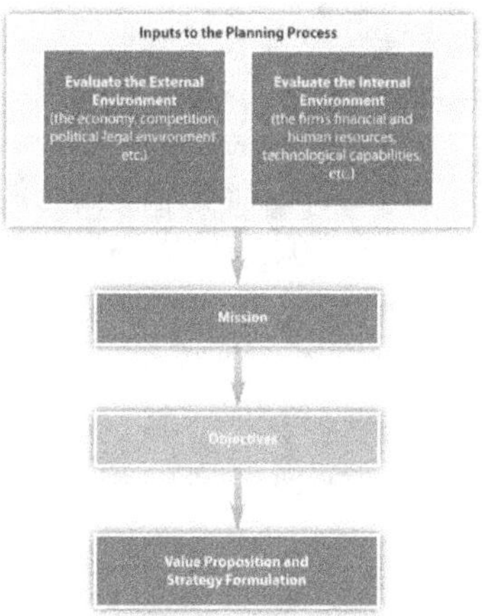

Purposes or Missions

Identifies the basic task of a firm or agency.Ex. Purpose of business is the production anddistribution of goods and services

Dupont - Better things through chemistry

Kleenex - Production and sale of paper & products

Hallmark - Social expression of business

J & J - First responsibility to doctors, nurses, patients and mothers

Dow chemical - Sharing world's obligation for the protection of the environment

Conglomerates express their mission as 'synergy' which is achieved through combination of avariety of companies.

Therefore mission is the organization's purpose and fundamental reason for existence. Amission statement is the broad declaration of the basic. Unique purpose and scope of operationsdistinguish the organization from others.

Objectives and Goals

Planning aims at goal setting. Goals and objectives are ends towards the activity aimed. Theyrepresent the end toward organizing, staffing, leading and controlling. Each department mayhave its own goals, which contribute to objectives of organizations as illustrated below.

Mission

The purpose of a mission statement is to give a concise explanation of the business's reason for existing and its long-term goals.

A company's mission describes what the company does. It describes why an organization is operating and thus provides a framework within which strategies are formulated. It describes what the organization does (i.e., present capabilities), who all it serves (i.e., stakeholders) and what makes an organization unique (i.e., reason for existence). A mission statement differentiates an organization from others by explaining its broad scope of activities, its products, and technologies it uses to achieve its goals and objectives. It talks about an organization's present (i.e., -about where we are).

Ex: Microsoft's mission is to help people and businesses throughout the world to realize their full potential.

Elements of a Mission Statement

Function

The mission statement needs to include some description of the function of the business. For example, "to promote industrial excellence," tells customers and employees nothing. A more effective description would be "To provide management consulting services."

Target Consumers

An effective mission statement sets out, in broad terms, the target market. A manufacturer that makes nuts and bolts might set its target market as retail hardware stores, machine manufacturers, or both.

Target Region

The business must determine what region it serves best and relay that information by way of the mission statement. A garage, for example, might limit its target region to the community while a magazine company might target an entire country.

Values

Mission statements typically include a statement of company values. Values such as customer service, efficiency and eco-consciousness often appear on lists of company values. At their best, company values should express principles the company explicitly tries to affirm in day-to-day operations.

Technology

For businesses that rely heavily on technology, the mission statement should include a description of the essential technology the company does or plans to employ. If nothing else, this directs purchasing agents toward the appropriate vendors for goods and services.

Employees

Every company has a policy regarding its relationship with employees. A mission statement provides an opportunity to describe that policy in brief so employees know the essentials of where they stand.

Strategic Positioning

Effective mission statements also include a brief description of the business's strategic position within the market. For example, the company might excel at serving residential clients and seek to maximize that strategic advantage.

Financial Objectives

For for-profit ventures, businesses require clear financial objectives. A start-up company might set one of its financial objectives as making an initial public offering of common stock within two years. This lets the employees and potential investors know the company intends to go public, with all of the legal and record keeping ramifications that entails.

Image

Like people, companies develop public images. Careful companies craft the public image they want to establish and lay out the major features of it in the mission statement. This helps managers direct employees that stray from the sanctioned public image.

Importance of Mission

1. It Determines the Company's Direction

Smart business owners use this statement to remind their teams why their company exists because this is what makes the company successful. The mission statement serves as a "North Star" that keeps everyone clear on the direction of the organization. And as Andy Stanley says, "It's your direction, not your intention, that determines your destination." This leads to the second reason.

2. It Focuses the Company's Future

Many people refer to this as the "vision" which is different than the mission. The vision is about a preferred future. Where will you be in 1 year? 3 years? 5 years? The mission tells us what we're doing today that will then take us where we want to go in the future.

3. It Provides a Template for Decision-making

A clear mission sets important boundaries which enable business owners to delegate both responsibility and authority. Mission is to the company what a compass is to an explorer, a map to a tourist, a rudder to a ship, a template to a machinist. It provides a framework for thinking throughout the organization. It provides the boundaries and guardrails you need in order to stay on the path to your preferred future.

4. It Forms the Basis for Alignment

When a new employee is hired, it's critical that the new hire know what the company does and where the company is going. The mission statement forms the basis for alignment not only with the owner, but the entire team and organization. Your team will all be on the same page when it comes to what you do and why you do it, which leads to better effectiveness and efficiency.

5. It Welcomes Helpful Change

Many people are resistant to change because it causes us to feel insecure and sometimes out of control. However, if the mission is clear, then team members are more likely to see the value of the change and how it helps the organization accomplish the mission. This will create a culture that welcomes change when warranted.

6. It Shapes Strategy

Every business and business owner need a strategy. But strategies must not be created in a vacuum. Instead of looking at what's new or what competitors are doing and trying to copy them, wise business owners create the most effective strategies possible to accomplish the mission their company is set out to accomplish.

7. It Facilitates Evaluation and Improvement

It has been said that "What you measure will be your mission." If there is a clear, written statement of mission we can know exactly what to measure and how to measure it.

Formulation of a Mission Statement

Mission statement has three main components-a statements of mission or vision of the company, a statement of the core values that shape the acts and behaviour of the employees, and a statement of the goals and objectives.Mission statements always exist at top level of an organization, but may also be made for various organizational levels. Chief executive plays a significant role in formulation of mission statement. Once the mission statement is formulated, it serves the organization in long run, but it may become ambiguous with organizational growth and innovations.

In today's dynamic and competitive environment, mission may need to be redefined. However, care must be taken that the redefined mission statement should have original fundamentals/components.

Needs/Features of a Mission

1. Mission must be feasible and attainable. It should be possible to achieve it.
2. Mission should be clear enough so that any action can be taken.
3. It should be inspiring for the management, staff and society at large.
4. It should be precise enough, i.e., it should be neither too broad nor too narrow.
5. It should be unique and distinctive to leave an impact in everyone's mind.
6. It should be analytical, i.e., it should analyse the key components of the strategy.
7. It should be credible, i.e., all stakeholders should be able to believe it.

Vision

A vision statement identifies where the organization wants or intends to be in future or where it should be to best meet the needs of the stakeholders. It describes dreams and aspirations for future. For instance, Microsoft's vision is —to empower people through great software, any time, any place, or any device.

A vision is the potential to view things ahead of themselves. It answers the question -where we want to be. It gives us a reminder about what we attempt to develop. A vision statement is for the organization and its members, unlike the mission statement which is for the customers/clients. It contributes in effective decision making as well as effective business planning. It incorporates a shared understanding about the nature and aim of the organization and utilizes this understanding to direct and guide the organization towards a better purpose. It describes that on achieving the mission, how the organizational future would appear to be.

Features of an Effective Vision Statement must have Following

1. It must be unambiguous
2. It must be clear
3. It must harmonize with organization's culture and values
4. The dreams and aspirations must be rational/realistic
5. Vision statements should be shorter so that they are easier to memorize

Objectives

Objectives are defined as goals that organization wants to achieve over a period of time. These are the foundation of planning. Policies are developed in an organization so as to achieve these objectives. Formulation of objectives is the task of top level management.

Features of Effective Objectives must have the Following

1. These are not single for an organization, but multiple
2. Objectives should be both short-term as well as long-term
3. Objectives must respond and react to changes in environment, i.e., they must be flexible
4. These must be feasible, realistic and operational

In general, an organization should have 3 types of Objectives:

1. Short Term Objectives: Targets to be achieved in 1 year or less
2. Intermediate Term Objectives: Targets to be achieved in 1 to 5 years
3. Long Term Objectives: Targets to be achieved in 5 to 7 years

Areas where objectives are set:

- Growth
- Profitability
- Market share
- Productivity
- Technology
- R&D
- CSR
- Employee Satisfaction

Guidelines for Establishing Objectives

1. Let the people responsible for attaining the objectives have a voice in setting them
2. State Objective as specifically as possible
3. Relate objectives to specific actions whenever necessary
4. Pinpoint expected results
5. Set goals high enough that employees have to strive to meet them, but not so high that employees give up trying to meet them
6. Specify when goals are expected to be achieved
7. Set objectives only in relation to other organizational objectives
8. State Objectives clearly and simply

Characteristics

Specific

Instead of stating objectives as growth in assets, sales and profits, it is better to state specifically that 12% increase in sales, 10% in profits, etc,.

Time Bound

The time frame for the specific objectives has to be mentioned by month or year according to the objective framed.

Measurable

The objectives should be measured and compared with best companies in the industry.

Challenging

Objectives should be attainable and realistic but challenging for the employees. Targets shouldn't be dangerous and mislead the employees and result in frustration and sub optimal performance.

Objectives form a Hierarchy

Objectives are structured in a hierarchy of importance. There are objectives within objectives. The objectives of each unit contribute to the objectives of the next higher unit. Hence no work should be undertaken unless it contributes to the overall objective.

Constraints

External constraints like consumer activism, WTO, pollution control, etc., and internal constraints like shortage of materials, labour, etc., serve as a limitation to objective setting.

Verifiable

Verifiable objectives are measurable irrespective of their qualitative nature. In order to measure objectives should be quantified. Quantifiable objectives alone should be set in strategic management.

Timeframe

Objectives are framed for different time periods such as long term, medium term and short term, such objectives should be integrated with each other.

Formulation of Objectives

The Forces in the Environment

The government regulations, powerful consumer groups, trade unions and influential suppliers exert enormous pressure on organisation. The stake holders, their priorities and views influence objective setting.

Realities of Firm's Resources and Power Relationship

Material and human resource are always scarce and powerful dominant groups try to take upper hand and exercise power over other groups in framing objectives of their choice and allocate scarce resources in their favour. Internal power relationship influences objective setting.

The Values of Top Management

Values are enduring beliefs about what is good or bad, desirable or undesirable. The top management may have entrepreneurial value or a philanthropic value or social responsibility value which in turn will influence their goal setting.

Past Strategies

Strategies and objectives are followed in the recent past is likely to have deep impact and radical deviation from them will not be possible. The changes from current objectives will be marginal and incremental in nature.

Goals

A goal is a desired future state or objective that an organization tries to achieve. Goals specify in particular what must be done if an organization is to attain mission or vision. Goals make mission more prominent and concrete. They co-ordinate and integrate various functional and departmental areas in an organization.

Features

1. These are precise and measurable
2. These look after critical and significant issues
3. These are realistic and challenging
4. These must be achieved within a specific time frame
5. These include both financial as well as non-financial components

Types

Difference in goals required because of the organization's level, area or department, and time frame. Based on these three criteria's goals can be categorized in three types;

- Strategic Goals
- Tactical Goals, and
- Operational Goals

They are described below

Strategic Goals

Strategic goals are goals set by and for top management of the organization. These goals are made by focusing on broad general issues. Strategic goals or strategy are usually long-term and from this goal other goals are made and set for different time-frames and area.

Tactical Goals

Tactical goals are set for middle managers. These goals focus on how to operationalize actions necessary to achieve the strategic goals. Middle managers of various departments are usually responsible for their attainment. Tactical goals are set by the middle managers, but often top-managers set tactical goals for the middle managers.

Operational Goals

Operational goals are set by and for lower-level managers. Operational goals are usually made to tackle shorter-term issues associated with the tactical goals and lower-managers are responsible for their attainment.

The three levels of goals within an organization form a hierarchy of goals, with lower-level goals forming a mean-end chain with the next level of goals.

CHAPTER II

EXTERNAL ENVIRONMENT

2.1. Environmental Analysis

Environmental analysis is a strategic tool. It is a process to identify all the external and internal elements, which can affect the organization's performance. The analysis entails assessing the level of threat or opportunity the factors might present. These evaluations are later translated into the decision-making process. The analysis helps align strategies with the firm's environment.

2.2. Environmental Scanning

Organizational environment consists of both external and internal factors. Environment must be scanned so as to determine development and forecasts of factors that will influence organizational success. Environmental scanning refers to possession and utilization of information about occasions, patterns, trends, and relationships within an organization's internal and external environment. It helps the managers to decide the future path of the organization. Scanning must identify the threats and opportunities existing in the environment. While strategy formulation, an organization must take advantage of the opportunities and minimize the threats. A threat for one organization may be an opportunity for another.

Internal analysis of the environment is the first step of environment scanning. Organizations should observe the internal organizational environment. This includes employee interaction with other employees, employee interaction with management, manager interaction with other managers, and management interaction with shareholders, access to natural resources, brand awareness, organizational structure, main staff, operational potential, etc. Also, discussions, interviews, and surveys can be used to assess the internal environment. Analysis of internal environment helps in identifying strengths and weaknesses of an organization.

As business becomes more competitive, and there are rapid changes in the external environment, information from external environment adds crucial elements to the effectiveness of long-term plans. As environment is dynamic, it becomes essential to identify competitors' moves and actions. Organizations have also to update the core competencies and internal environment as per external environment. Environmental factors are infinite, hence, organization should be agile and vigile to accept and adjust to the environmental changes. For instance - Monitoring might indicate that an original forecast of the prices of the raw materials that are involved in the product are no more credible, which could imply the requirement for more focused scanning, forecasting and analysis to create a more trustworthy prediction about the input costs. In a similar manner, there can be changes in factors such as competitor's activities, technology, market tastes and preferences.

While in external analysis, three correlated environment should be studied and analyzed:

- immediate/industry environment
- national environment
- broader socio-economic environment/macro-environment

Examining the industry environment needs an appraisal of the competitive structure of the organization's industry, including the competitive position of a particular organization and it's main rivals. Also, an assessment of the nature, stage, dynamics and history of the industry is essential. It also implies evaluating the effect of globalization on competition within the industry. Analyzing the national environment needs an appraisal of whether the national framework helps in achieving competitive advantage in the globalized environment. Analysis of macro-environment includes exploring macro-economic, social, government, legal, technological and international factors that may influence the environment. The analysis of organization's external environment reveals opportunities and threats for an organization.

Strategic managers must not only recognize the present state of the environment and their industry but also be able to predict its future positions.

Our market is facing changes every day. Many new things develop over time and the whole scenario can alter in only a few seconds. There are some factors that are beyond your control. But, you can control a lot of these things.

Businesses are greatly influenced by their environment. All the situational factors which determine day to day circumstances impact firms. So, businesses must constantly analyze the trade environment and the market.There are many strategic analysis tools that a firm can use.

2.3. Situational Analysis

A systematic collection and evaluation of past and present economical, political, social, and technological data, aimed at (1) identification of internal and external forces that may influence the organization's performance and choice of strategies, and (2) assessment of the organization's current and future strengths, weaknesses, opportunities, and threats.

PEST/ PESTLE

PESTLE analysis consists of various factors that affect the business environment. Each letter in the acronym signifies a set of factors. These factors can affect every industry directly or indirectly.The letters in PESTLE, also called PESTEL, denote the following things:

- Political factors
- Economic factors
- Social factors
- Technological factors
- Legal factors
- Environmental factor

Often, managers choose to learn about political, economic, social and technological factors only. In that case, they conduct the PEST analysis. PEST is also an environmental analysis. It is a shorter version of PESTLE analysis. STEP, STEEP, STEEPLE, STEEPLED, STEPJE and LEPEST: All of these are acronyms for the same set of factors. Some of them gauge additional factors like ethical and demographical factors.

The 6 most commonly assessed factors in environmental analysis are:

P for Political Factors

The political factors take the country's current political situation. It also reads the global political condition's effect on the country and business.

When conducting this step, ask questions like "What kind of government leadership is impacting decisions of the firm?"

Some political factors that you can study are:

- Government policies
- Taxes laws and tariff
- Stability of government
- Entry mode regulations

E for Economic Factors

Economic factors involve all the determinants of the economy and its state. These are factors that can conclude the direction in which the economy might move. So, businesses analyze this factor based on the environment. It helps to set up strategies in line with changes.

I have listed some determinants you can assess to know how economic factors are affecting your business below:

- The inflation rate
- The interest rate
- Disposable income of buyers
- Credit accessibility
- Unemployment rates
- The monetary or fiscal policies
- The foreign exchange rate

S for Social Factors

Countries vary from each other. Every country has a distinctive mindset. These attitudes have an impact on the businesses. The social factors might ultimately affect the sales of products and services.

Some of the social factors you should study are:

- The cultural implications
- The gender and connected demographics
- The social lifestyles
- The domestic structures
- Educational levels
- Distribution of Wealth

T for Technological Factors

Technology is advancing continuously. The advancement is greatly influencing businesses. Performing environmental analysis on these factors will help you stay up to date with the changes. Technology alters every minute. This is why companies must stay connected all the time. Firms should integrate when needed. Technological factors will help you know how the consumers react to various trends.

Firms can use these factors for their benefit:

- New discoveries
- Rate of technological obsolescence
- Rate of technological advances
- Innovative technological platforms

L for Legal Factors

Legislative changes take place from time to time. Many of these changes affect the business environment. If a regulatory body sets up a regulation for industries, for example, that law would impact industries and business in that economy. So, businesses should also analyze the legal developments in respective environments.

I have mentioned some legal factors you need to be aware of:

- Product regulations
- Employment regulations
- Competitive regulations
- Patent infringements
- Health and safety regulations

E for Environmental Factors

The location influences business trades. Changes in climatic changes can affect the trade. The consumer reactions to particular offering can also be an issue. This most often affects agri-businesses.

Some environmental factors you can study are:

- Geographical location
- The climate and weather
- Waste disposal laws
- Energy consumption regulation
- People's attitude towards the environment

There are many external factors other than the ones mentioned above. None of these factors are independent. They rely on each other.

If you are wondering how you can conduct environmental analysis, here are 5 simple steps you could follow:

- Understand all the environmental factors before moving to the next step.
- Collect all the relevant information.
- Identify the opportunities for your organization.
- Recognize the threats your company faces.
- The final step is to take action.

It is true that industry factors have an impact on the company performance. Environmental analysis is essential to determine what role certain factors play in your business. PEST or PESTLE analysis allows businesses to take a look at the external factors. Many organizations use these tools to project the growth of their company effectively.

The analyses provide a good look at factors like revenue, profitability, and corporate success. If you want to take the right decisions for your firm, employ environmental analysis. The analysis you should conduct depends on the nature of your company.

2.4.   Porter's Five Forces Model

Porter's five forces model is an analysis tool that uses five industry forces to determine the intensity of competition in an industry and its profitability level.

Five forces model was created by M. Porter in 1979 to understand how five key competitive forces are affecting an industry. The five forces identified are:

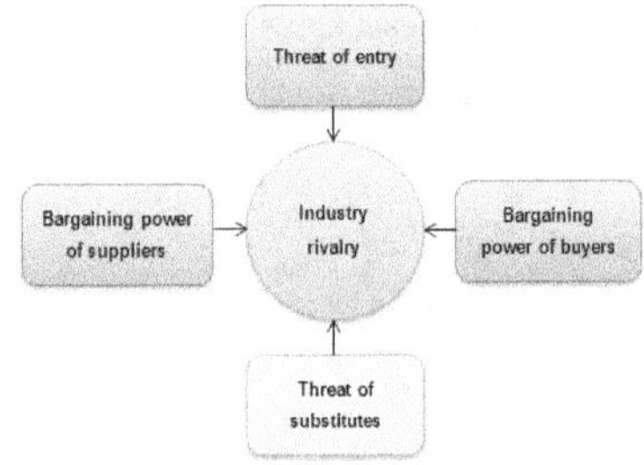

These forces determine an industry structure and the level of competition in that industry. The stronger competitive forces in the industry are the less profitable it is. An industry with low barriers to enter, having few buyers and suppliers but many substitute products and competitors will be seen as very competitive and thus, not so attractive due to its low profitability.

It is every strategist's job to evaluate company's competitive position in the industry and to identify what strengths or weakness can be exploited to strengthen that position. The tool is very useful in formulating firm's strategy as it reveals how powerful each of the five key forces is in a particular industry.

Threat of new entrants. This force determines how easy (or not) it is to enter a particular industry. If an industry is profitable and there are few barriers to enter, rivalry soon intensifies. When more organizations compete for the same market share, profits start to fall. It is essential for existing organizations to create high barriers to enter to deter new entrants. Threat of new entrants is high when:

- Low amount of capital is required to enter a market
- Existing companies can do little to retaliate
- Existing firms do not possess patents, trademarks or do not have established brand reputation
- There is no government regulation
- Customer switching costs are low (it doesn't cost a lot of money for a firm to switch to other industries)
- There is low customer loyalty
- Products are nearly identical
- Economies of scale can be easily achieved.

Bargaining power of suppliers. Strong bargaining power allows suppliers to sell higher priced or low quality raw materials to their buyers. This directly affects the buying firms' profits because it has to pay more for materials.

Suppliers have strong bargaining power when:

- There are few suppliers but many buyers
- Suppliers are large and threaten to forward integrate
- Few substitute raw materials exist
- Suppliers hold scarce resources
- Cost of switching raw materials is especially high

Bargaining power of buyers. Buyers have the power to demand lower price or higher product quality from industry producers when their bargaining power is strong. Lower price means lower revenues for the producer, while higher quality products usually raise production costs. Both scenarios result in lower profits for producers.

Buyers exert strong bargaining power when:

- Buying in large quantities or control many access points to the final customer
- Only few buyers exist
- Switching costs to other supplier are low
- They threaten to backward integrate
- There are many substitutes
- Buyers are price sensitive

Threat of substitutes. This force is especially threatening when buyers can easily find substitute products with attractive prices or better quality and when buyers can switch from one product or service to another with little cost. For example, to switch from coffee to tea doesn't cost anything, unlike switching from car to bicycle.

Rivalry among existing competitors. This force is the major determinant on how competitive and profitable an industry is. In competitive industry, firms have to compete aggressively for a market share, which results in low profits. Rivalry among competitors is intense when:

- There are many competitors
- Exit barriers are high
- Industry of growth is slow or negative
- Products are not differentiated and can be easily substituted
- Competitors are of equal size
- Low customer loyalty

Although, Porter originally introduced five forces affecting an industry, scholars have suggested including the sixth force: **complements**. Complements increase the demand of the primary product with which they are used, thus, increasing firm's and industry's profit potential. For example, iTunes was created to complement iPod and added value for both products. As a result, both iTunes and iPod sales increased, increasing Apple's profits.

Using the Tool

We now understand that Porter's five forces framework is used to analyze industry's competitive forces and to shape organization's strategy according to the results of the analysis. But how to use this tool? We have identified the following steps:

- Step 1. Gather the information on each of the five forces
- Step 2. Analyze the results and display them on a diagram
- Step 3. Formulate strategies based on the conclusions

Step 1. Gather the information on each of the five forces. What managers should do during this step is to gather information about their industry and to check it against each of the factors (such as "number of competitors in the industry") influencing the force. We have already identified the most important factors given below.

Porter's Five Forces Factors

Threat of New Entry

- Amount of capital required
- Retaliation by existing companies
- Legal barriers (patents, copyrights, etc.)
- Brand reputation
- Product differentiation
- Access to suppliers and distributors
- Economies of scale
- Sunk costs
- Government regulation

Supplier Power

- Number of suppliers
- Suppliers' size
- Ability to find substitute materials
- Materials scarcity
- Cost of switching to alternative materials
- Threat of integrating forward

Buyer Power

- Number of buyers
- Size of buyers
- Size of each order
- Buyers' cost of switching suppliers
- There are many substitutes
- Price sensitivity
- Threat of integrating backward

Threat of Substitutes

- Number of substitutes
- Performance of substitutes
- Cost of changing

Rivalry among Existing Competitors

- Number of competitors
- Cost of leaving an industry
- Industry growth rate and size
- Product differentiation
- Competitors' size
- Customer loyalty
- Threat of horizontal integration
- Level of advertising expense

Step 2. Analyze the results and display them on a diagram. After gathering all the information, you should analyze it and determine how each force is affecting an industry. For example, if there are many companies of equal size operating in the slow growth industry, it means that rivalry between existing companies is strong. Remember that five forces affect different industries differently so don't use the same results of analysis for even similar industries!

Step 3. Formulate strategies based on the conclusions. At this stage, managers should formulate firm's strategies using the results of the analysis For example, if it is hard to achieve economies of scale in the market, the company should pursue cost leadership strategy. Product development strategy should be used if the current market growth is slow and the market is saturated.

Although, Porter's five forces is a great tool to analyze industry's structure and use the results to formulate firm's strategy, it has its limitations and requires further analysis to be done, such as SWOT, PEST or Value Chain analysis.

2.5.   SWOT Analysis

A scan of the internal and external environment is an important part of the strategicplanning process. Environmental factors internal to the firm usually can be classified asstrengths (**S**) or weaknesses (**W**), and those external to the firm can be classified asopportunities (**O**) or threats (**T**). Such an analysis of the strategic environment is referredto as a SWOT analysis.

The SWOT analysis provides information that is helpful in matching the firm's resourcesand capabilities to the competitive environment in which it operates. As such, it isinstrumental in strategy formulation and selection.

Strengths

A firm's strengths are its resources and capabilities that can be used as a basis fordeveloping a competitive advantage.

Examples of such strengths include:

- patents
- strong brand names
- good reputation among customers
- cost advantages from proprietary know-how
- exclusive access to high grade natural resources
- favorable access to distribution networks

Weaknesses

The absence of certain strengths may be viewed as a weakness.

For example, each of thefollowing may be considered weaknesses:

- lack of patent protection
- a weak brand name
- poor reputation among customers
- high cost structure
- lack of access to the best natural resources
- lack of access to key distribution channels

In some cases, a weakness may be the flip side of a strength. Take the case in which afirm has a large amount of manufacturing capacity. While this capacity may beconsidered a strength that competitors do not share, it also may be a considered aweakness if the large investment in manufacturing capacity prevents the firm fromreacting quickly to changes in the strategic environment.

Opportunities

The external environmental analysis may reveal certain new opportunities for profitand growth. Some examples of such opportunities include:

- an unfulfilled customer need
- arrival of new technologies
- loosening of regulations
- removal of international trade barriers

Threats

Changes in the external environmental also may present threats to the firm. Someexamples of such threats include:

- shifts in consumer tastes away from the firm's products
- emergence of substitute products
- new regulations
- increased trade barriers

The SWOT Matrix

A firm should not necessarily pursue the more lucrative opportunities. Rather, it mayhave a better chance at developing a competitive advantage by identifying a fit betweenthe firm's strengths and upcoming opportunities. In some cases, the firm can overcome aweakness in order to prepare itself to pursue a compelling opportunity.

To develop strategies that take into account the SWOT profile, a matrix of these factorscan be constructed. The SWOT matrix (also known as a **TOWS Matrix**) isshown below:

2.6. SWOT/TOWS Matrix

	Strengths	Weakness
Opportunities	S-O Strategies	W-O Strategies
Threats	S-T Strategies	W-T Strategies

S-O strategies pursue opportunities that are a good fit to the company's strengths.

- **W-O strategies** overcome weaknesses to pursue opportunities.
- **S-T strategies** identify ways that the firm can use its strengths to reduce itsvulnerability to external threats.
- **W-T strategies** establish a defensive plan to prevent the firm's weaknesses frommaking it highly susceptible to external threats.

2.7. Environmental Threat and Opportunity Profile (ETOP)

The Environmental factors are quite complex and it may be difficult for strategy managers to classify them into neat categories to interpret them as opportunities and threats. A matrix of comparison is drawn where one item or factor is compared with other items after which the scores arrived at are added and ranked for each factor and total weight age score calculated for prioritizing each of the factors.

This is achieved by brainstorming. And finally the strategy manger uses his judgment to place various environmental issues in clear perspective to create the environmental threat and opportunity profile.

Although the technique of dividing various environmental factors into specific sectors and evaluating them as opportunities and threats is suggested by some authors, it must be carefully noted that each sector is not exclusive of the other.

Each of the major factors pertaining to a particular sector of environment may be divided into sub-sectors and their effects studied. The field force analysis goes hand in glove with ETOP, as here also the contribution with regard to opportunities and threats posed by the environment is also a necessary part of study.

ETOP Preparation

The preparation of ETOP involves dividing the environment into different sectors and then analyzing the impact of each sector on the organization. A comprehensive ETOP requires subdividing each environmental sector into sub factors and then the impact of each sub factor on the organization is described in the form of a statement.

A summary ETOP may only show the major factors for the sake of simplicity. The table 1 provides an example of an ETOP prepared for an established company, which is in the Two Wheeler industry.

The main business of the company is in Motor Bike manufacturing for the domestic and exports markets.

This example relates to a hypothetical company but the illustration is realistic based n the current Indian business environment.

Table 1: Environmental Threat and Opportunity Profile (ETOP) for a Motor Bike Company

Environmental Sectors	Impact of each sector
Social ($\uparrow$)	Customer preference for motorbike, which are fashionable, easy to ride and durable.
Political ($\rightarrow$)	No significant factor.
Economic ($\uparrow$)	Growing affluence among urban consumers; Exports potential high.
Regulatory ($\uparrow$)	Two Wheeler industry a thrust area for exports.
Market ($\uparrow$)	Industry growth rate is 10 to 12 percent per year, For motorbike growth rate is 40 percent, largely Unsaturated demand.
Supplier ($\uparrow$)	Mostly ancillaries and associated companies supply parts and components, REP licenses for imported raw materials available.
Technological ($\uparrow$)	Technological up gradation of industry in progress. Import of machinery under OGL list possible.

As shown in the table motorbike manufacturing is an attractive proposition due to the many opportunities operating in the environment. The company-can capitalize on the burgeoning demand by taking advantage of the various government policies and concessions. It can also take advantage of the high exports potential that already exists.

Since the company is an established manufacturer of motorbike, it has a favorable supplier as well as technological environment. But contrast the implications of this ETOP for a new manufacturer who is planning to enter this industry.

Though the market environment would still be favorable, much would depend on the extent to which the company is able to ensure the supply of raw materials and components, and have access to the latest technology and have the facilities to use it. The preparation of an ETOP provides a clear picture for organization to formulate strategies to take advantage of the opportunities and counter the threats in its environment.

The strategic managers should keep focus on the following dimensions,

1. Issue Selection
2. Accuracy of Data
3. Impact Studies
4. Flexibility in Operations

2.8. Value Chain Analysis (VCA)

VCA is a process where a firm identifies its primary and support activities that add value to its final product and then analyze these activities to reduce costs or increase differentiation.

Value chainrepresents the internal activities a firm engages in when transforming inputs into outputs.

Understanding the Tool

Value chain analysis is a strategy tool used to analyze internal firm activities. Its goal is to recognize, which activities are the most valuable (i.e. are the source of cost or differentiation advantage) to the firm and which ones could be improved to provide competitive advantage. In other words, by looking into internal activities, the analysis reveals where a firm's competitive advantages or disadvantages are. The firm that competes through differentiation advantage will try to perform its activities better than competitors would do. If it competes through cost advantage, it will try to perform internal activities at lower costs than competitors would do. When a company is capable of producing goods at lower costs than the market price or to provide superior products, it earns profits.

M. Porter introduced the generic value chain model in 1985. Value chain represents all the internal activities a firm engages in to produce goods and services. VC is formed of primary activities that add value to the final product directly and support activities that add value indirectly.

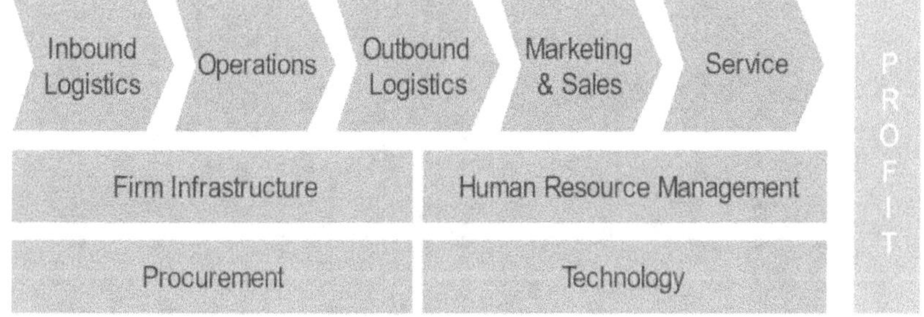

Although, primary activities add value directly to the production process, they are not necessarily more important than support activities. Nowadays, competitive advantage mainly derives from technological improvements or innovations in business models or processes. Therefore, such support activities as 'information systems', 'R&D' or 'general management' are usually the most important source of differentiation advantage. On the other hand, primary activities are usually the source of cost advantage, where costs can be easily identified for each activity and properly managed.

Firm's VC is a part of a larger industry VC. The more activities a company undertakes compared to industry VC, the more vertically integrated it is. Below you can find an industry value chain and its relation to a firm level VC.

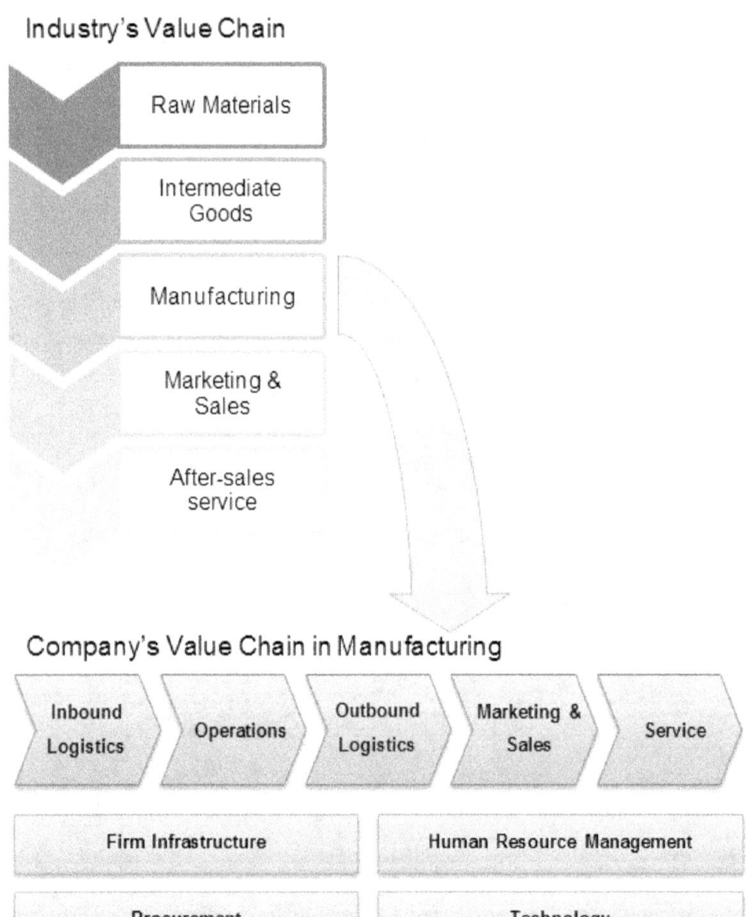

Using the Tool

There are two different approaches on how to perform the analysis, which depend on what type of competitive advantage a company wants to create (cost or differentiation advantage). The table below lists all the steps needed to achieve cost or differentiation advantage using VCA.

2.9. Competitive Advantage

Competitive advantage	
Types	
Cost advantage	**Differentiation advantage**
This approach is used when organizations try to compete on costs and want to understand the sources of their cost advantage or disadvantage and what factors drive those costs.	The firms that strive to create superior products or services use differentiation advantage approach.
• Step 1. Identify the firm's primary and support activities. • Step 2. Establish the relative importance of each activity in the total cost of the product. • Step 3. Identify cost drivers for each activity. • Step 4. Identify links between activities. • Step 5. Identify opportunities for reducing costs.	• Step 1. Identify the customers' value-creating activities. • Step 2. Evaluate the differentiation strategies for improving customer value. • Step 3. Identify the best sustainable differentiation.

Cost Advantage

To gain cost advantage a firm has to go through 5 analysis steps:

Step 1. Identify the firm's primary and support activities. All the activities (from receiving and storing materials to marketing, selling and after sales support) that are undertaken to produce goods or services have to be clearly identified and separated from each other. This requires an adequate knowledge of company's operations because value chain activities are not organized in the same way as the company itself. The managers who identify value chain activities have to look into how work is done to deliver customer value.

Step 2. Establish the relative importance of each activity in the total cost of the product. The total costs of producing a product or service must be broken down and assigned to each activity. Activity based costing is used to calculate costs for each process. Activities that are the major sources of cost or done inefficiently (when benchmarked against competitors) must be addressed first.

Step 3. Identify cost drivers for each activity. Only by understanding what factors drive the costs, managers can focus on improving them. Costs for labor-intensive activities will be driven by work hours, work speed, wage rate, etc. Different activities will have different cost drivers.

Step 4. Identify links between activities. Reduction of costs in one activity may lead to further cost reductions in subsequent activities. For example, fewer components in the product design may lead to less faulty parts and lower service costs. Therefore identifying the links between activities will lead to better understanding how cost improvements would affect he whole value chain. Sometimes, cost reductions in one activity lead to higher costs for other activities.

Step 5. Identify opportunities for reducing costs. When the company knows its inefficient activities and cost drivers, it can plan on how to improve them. Too high wage rates can be dealt with by increasing production speed, outsourcing jobs to low wage countries or installing more automated processes.

Differentiation Advantage

VCA is done differently when a firm competes on differentiation rather than costs. This is because the source of differentiation advantage comes from creating superior products, adding more features and satisfying varying customer needs, which results in higher cost structure.

Step 1. Identify the customers' value-creating activities. After identifying all value chain activities, managers have to focus on those activities that contribute the most to creating customer value. For example, Apple products' success mainly comes not from great product features (other companies have high-quality offerings too) but from successful marketing activities.

Step 2. Evaluate the differentiation strategies for improving customer value. Managers can use the following strategies to increase product differentiation and customer value:

- Add more product features

- Focus on customer service and responsiveness

- Increase customization

- Offer complementary products.

Step 3. Identify the best sustainable differentiation. Usually, superior differentiation and customer value will be the result of many interrelated activities and strategies used. The best combination of them should be used to pursue sustainable differentiation advantage.

Example

This example is partially adopted from R. M. Grant's book 'Contemporary Strategy Analysis' p.241. It illustrates the basic VCA for an automobile manufacturing company that competes on cost advantage. This analysis doesn't include support activities that are essential to any firm's value chain, thus the analysis itself is not complete.

Value Chain Analysis Example					
Step 1 - Firm's primary activities					
Design and engineering	Purchasing materials and components	Assembly	Testing and quality control	Sales and marketing	Distribution and dealer support
Step 2 - Total cost and importance					
$164 M less important	$410 M very important	$524 M very important	$10 M not important	$384 M important	$230 M less important
Step 3 - Cost drivers					
Number andfrequency of new models Sales per model	Order size Average value of purchases per supplier Location of suppliers	Scale of plants Capacity utilization Location of plants	Level of quality targets Frequency of defects	Size of advertising budget Strength of existing reputation Sales Volume	Number of dealers Sales per dealer Frequency of defects requiring repair recalls
Step 4 - Links between activities					
1. High-quality assembling process reduces defects and costs in quality control and dealer support activities. 2. Locating plants near the cluster of suppliers or dealers reduces purchasing and distribution costs. 3. Fewer model designs reduce assembling costs. 4. Higher order sizes increase warehousing costs.					
Step 5 - Opportunities for reducing costs					
1. Create just one model design for different regions to cut costs in designing and engineering, to increase order sizes of the same materials, to simplify assembling and quality control processes and to lower marketing costs. 2. Manufacture components inside the company to eliminate transaction costs of buying them in the market and to optimize plant utilization. This would also lead to greater economies of scale.					

Competitive advantage refers to any factors that make potential customers choose one company over another to supply any item or service. Superior core competency is of course a competitive advantage, but only one of many. A few of many other competitive advantages might be:

- Lowest price
- Ability to deliver most promptly
- Being known to most potential customers, e.g. by advertizing
- Superior reputation, most likely due to superior past work
- Superior courtesy toward customers
- Bribes to those who make purchasing decisions

  (I didn't say they were all good.)

Core competency is the ability of a company (including possibly a company of one person) to do acceptably well the task for which the company is known. For example, the core competency of a company named "Joe's Car Service" is the ability to service cars acceptably well.

CHAPTER III

STRATEGIC ANALYSIS

3.1.   Strategic Choice

Definition

Strategic Choice involves a whole process through which a decision is taken to choose a particular option from various alternatives. There can be various methods through which the final choice can be selected upon. Managers and decision makers keep both the external and internal environment in mind before narrowing it down to one.

3.2.   BCG Matrix

Boston Consulting Group (BCG) Matrix is a four celled matrix (a 2 * 2 matrix) developed by BCG, USA. It is the most renowned corporate portfolio analysis tool. It provides a graphic representation for an organization to examine different businesses in it's portfolio on the basis of their related market share and industry growth rates. It is a two dimensional analysis on management of SBU's (Strategic Business Units). In other words, it is a comparative analysis of business potential and the evaluation of environment.

According to this matrix, business could be classified as high or low according to their industry growth rate and relative market share.

Relative Market Share = SBU Sales this year leading competitors sales this year.

Market Growth Rate = Industry sales this year - Industry Sales last year.

The analysis requires that both measures be calculated for each SBU. The dimension of business strength, relative market share, will measure comparative advantage indicated by market dominance. The key theory underlying this is existence of an experience curve and that market share is achieved due to overall cost leadership.

BCG matrix has four cells, with the horizontal axis representing relative market share and the vertical axis denoting market growth rate. The mid-point of relative market share is set at 1.0. if all the SBU's are in same industry, the average growth rate of the industry is used. While, if all the SBU's are located in different industries, then the mid-point is set at the growth rate for the economy.Resources are allocated to the business units according to their situation on the grid. The four cells of this matrix have been called as stars, cash cows, question marks and dogs. Each of these cells represents a particular type of business.

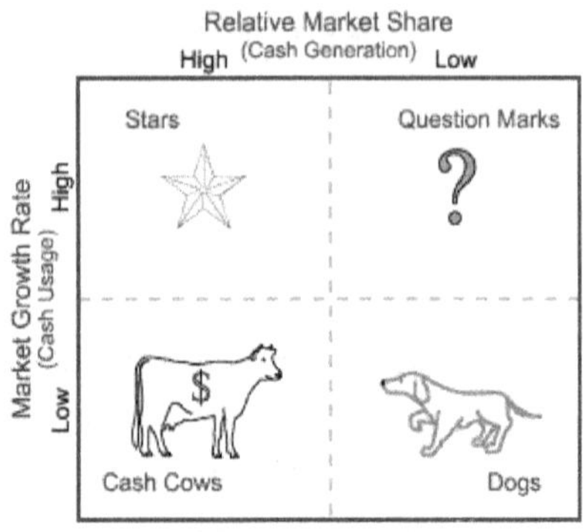

BCG Matrix

1. **Stars-** Stars represent business units having large market share in a fast growing industry. They may generate cash but because of fast growing market, stars require huge investments to maintain their lead. Net cash flow is usually modest. SBU's located in this cell are attractive as they are located in a robust industry and these business units are highly competitive in the industry. If successful, a star will become a cash cow when the industry matures.

2. **Cash Cows-** Cash Cows represents business units having a large market share in a mature, slow growing industry. Cash cows require little investment and generate cash that can be utilized for investment in other business units. These SBU's are the corporation's key source of cash, and are specifically the core business. They are the base of an organization. These businesses usually follow stability strategies. When cash cows loose their appeal and move towards deterioration, then a retrenchment policy may be pursued.

3. **Question Marks-** Question marks represent business units having low relative market share and located in a high growth industry. They require huge amount of cash to maintain or gain market share. They require attention to determine if the venture can be viable. Question marks are generally new goods and services which have a good commercial prospective. There is no specific strategy which can be adopted. If the firm thinks it has dominant market share, then it can adopt expansion strategy, else retrenchment strategy can be adopted. Most businesses start as question marks as the company tries to enter a high growth market in which there is already a market-share. If ignored, then question marks may become dogs, while if huge investment is made, then they have potential of becoming stars.

4. **Dogs**-Dogs represent businesses having weak market shares in low-growth markets. They neither generate cash nor require huge amount of cash. Due to low market share, these business units face cost disadvantages. Generally retrenchment strategies are adopted because these firms can gain market share only at the expense of competitor's/rival firms. These business firms have weak market share because of high costs, poor quality, ineffective marketing, etc. Unless a dog has some other strategic aim, it should be liquidated if there is fewer prospects for it to gain market share. Number of dogs should be avoided and minimized in an organization.

Limitations of BCG Matrix

The BCG Matrix produces a framework for allocating resources among different business units and makes it possible to compare many business units at a glance. But BCG Matrix is not free from limitations, such as-

1. BCG matrix classifies businesses as low and high, but generally businesses can be medium also. Thus, the true nature of business may not be reflected.
2. Market is not clearly defined in this model.
3. High market share does not always leads to high profits. There are high costs also involved with high market share.
4. Growth rate and relative market share are not the only indicators of profitability. This model ignores and overlooks other indicators of profitability.
5. At times, dogs may help other businesses in gaining competitive advantage. They can earn even more than cash cows sometimes.
6. This four-celled approach is considered as to be too simplistic.

3.3.   McKinsey 7s Model

McKinsey 7sis a tool that analyzes firm's organizational design by looking at 7 key internal elements: strategy, structure, systems, shared values, style, staff and skills, in order to identify if they are effectively aligned and allow organization to achieve its objectives.

McKinsey 7s model was developed in 1980s by McKinsey consultants Tom Peters, Robert Waterman and Julien Philips with a help from Richard Pascale and Anthony G. Athos. Since the introduction, the model has been widely used by academics and practitioners and remains one of the most popular strategic planning tools. It sought to present an emphasis on human resources (Soft S), rather than the traditional mass production tangibles of capital, infrastructure and equipment, as a key to higher organizational performance. The goal of the model was to show how 7 elements of the company: Structure, Strategy, Skills, Staff, Style, Systems, and Shared values, can be aligned together to achieve effectiveness in a company. The key point of the model is that all the seven areas are interconnected and a change in one area requires change in the rest of a firm for it to function effectively.

Below you can find the McKinsey model, which represents the connections between seven areas and divides them into 'Soft Ss' and 'Hard Ss'. The shape of the model emphasizes interconnectedness of the elements.

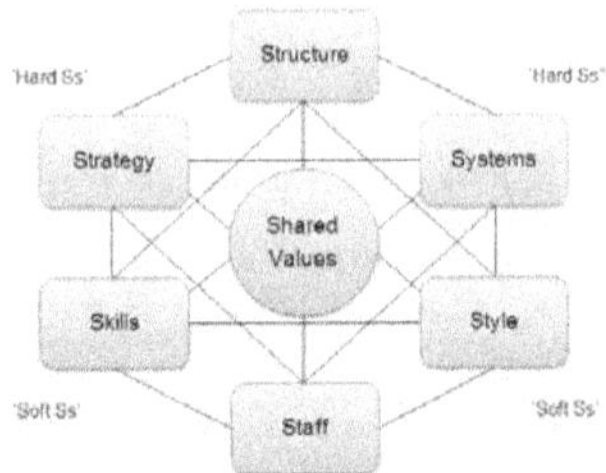

Source: https://www.strategicmanagementinsight.com/tools/mckinsey-7s-model-framework.html

The model can be applied to many situations and is a valuable tool when organizational design is at question. The most common uses of the framework are:

- To facilitate organizational change.
- To help implement new strategy.
- To identify how each area may change in a future.
- To facilitate the merger of organizations.

7s Factors

In McKinsey model, the seven areas of organization are divided into the 'soft' and 'hard' areas. Strategy, structure and systems are hard elements that are much easier to identify and manage when compared to soft elements. On the other hand, soft areas, although harder to manage, are the foundation of the organization and are more likely to create the sustained competitive advantage.

7s factors

Hard S	Soft S
Strategy	Style
Structure	Staff
Systems	Skills
	Shared Values

Strategy is a plan developed by a firm to achieve sustained competitive advantage and successfully compete in the market. What does a well-aligned strategy mean in 7s McKinsey model? In general, a sound strategy is the one that's clearly articulated, is long-term, helps to achieve competitive advantage and is reinforced by strong vision, mission and values. But it's hard to tell if such strategy is well-aligned with other elements when analyzed alone. So the key in 7s model is not to look at your company to find the great strategy, structure, systems and etc. but to look if its aligned with other elements. For example, short-term strategy is usually a poor choice for a company but if its aligned with other 6 elements, then it may provide strong results.

Structure represents the way business divisions and units are organized and includes the information of who is accountable to whom. In other words, structure is the organizational chart of the firm. It is also one of the most visible and easy to change elements of the framework.

Systems are the processes and procedures of the company, which reveal business' daily activities and how decisions are made. Systems are the area of the firm that determines how business is done and it should be the main focus for managers during organizational change.

Skills are the abilities that firm's employees perform very well. They also include capabilities and competences. During organizational change, the question often arises of what skills the company will really need to reinforce its new strategy or new structure.

Staff element is concerned with what type and how many employees an organization will need and how they will be recruited, trained, motivated and rewarded.

Style represents the way the company is managed by top-level managers, how they interact, what actions do they take and their symbolic value. In other words, it is the management style of company's leaders.

Shared Values are at the core of McKinsey 7s model. They are the norms and standards that guide employee behavior and company actions and thus, are the foundation of every organization.

Using the Tool

As we pointed out earlier, the McKinsey 7s framework is often used when organizational design and effectiveness are at question. It is easy to understand the model but much harder to apply it for your organization due to a common misunderstanding of what should a well-aligned elements be like.

We provide the following steps that should help you to apply this tool:

Step 1. Identify the areas that are not effectively aligned

During the first step, your aim is to look at the 7S elements and identify if they are effectively aligned with each other. Normally, you should already be aware of how 7 elements are aligned in your company, but if you don't you can use the checklist from WhittBlog to do that. After you've answered the questions outlined there you should look for the gaps, inconsistencies and weaknesses between the relationships of the elements. For example, you designed the strategy that relies on quick product introduction but the matrix structure with conflicting relationships hinders that so there's a conflict that requires the change in strategy or structure.

Step 2. Determine the optimal organization design

With the help from top management, your second step is to find out what effective organizational design you want to achieve. By knowing the desired alignment you can set your goals and make the action plans much easier. This step is not as straightforward as identifying how seven areas are currently aligned in your organization for a few reasons. First, you need to find the best optimal alignment, which is not known to you at the moment, so it requires more than answering the questions or collecting data. Second, there are no templates or predetermined organizational designs that you could use and you'll have to do a lot of research or benchmarking to find out how other similar organizations coped with organizational change or what organizational designs they are using.

Step 3. Decide where and what changes should be made

This is basically your action plan, which will detail the areas you want to realign and how would you like to do that. If you find that your firm's structure and management style are not aligned with company's values, you should decide how to reorganize the reporting relationships and which top managers should the company let go or how to influence them to change their management style so the company could work more effectively.

Step 4. Make the necessary changes

The implementation is the most important stage in any process, change or analysis and only the well-implemented changes have positive effects. Therefore, you should find the people in your company or hire consultants that are the best suited to implement the changes.

Step 5. Continuously review the 7s

The seven elements: strategy, structure, systems, skills, staff, style and values are dynamic and change constantly. A change in one element always has effects on the other elements and requires implementing new organizational design. Thus, continuous review of each area is very important.

3.4.   Strategic Gap Analysis

Gap Analysis refers to the comparison between what the performance was (actual) and what the performance should has been (potential). The results of this analysis help identify the errors in resource allocation and what steps need to be taken further to help improve performance through better utilization of the input resources.

The current performance is extrapolated back and compared with the desired performance level to get the results.

Gap= Current Performance- Desired Performance

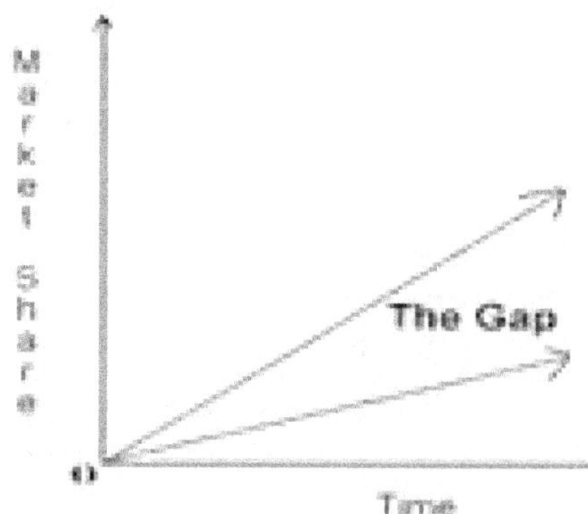

Strategic Gap Analysis helps identify performance gap with respect to the strategy the company follows to achieve its goals, whether the performance is aligned with the mission and vision of the company. This leads to resource optimization through the sages of determination, writing and application.

Strategic Gap = what the firm is doing - what the firm must do

The variance between the current and desired performance is an indicator of the gap in this case. The outcome is the identification of means to fill the gap.

GE Nine Cell Matrix

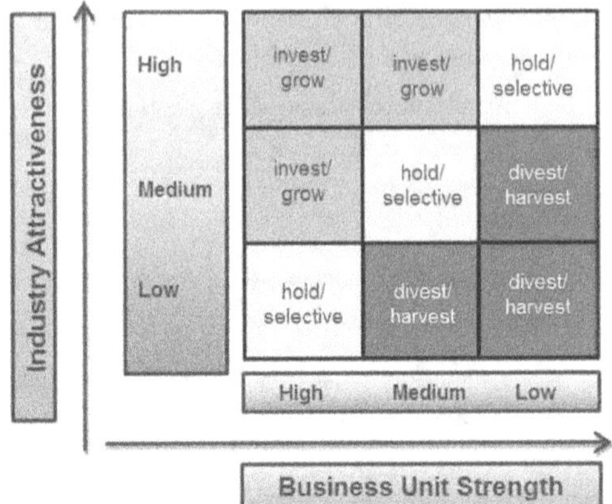

Another popular "Corporate Portfolio Analysis" technique is the result of pioneering effort of General Electric Company along with McKinsey Consultants which is known as the GE Nine Cell Matrix.

GE nine-box matrix is a strategy tool that offers a systematic approach for the multi business enterprises to prioritize their investments among the various business units. It is a framework that evaluates business portfolio and provides further strategic implications.

Each business is appraised in terms of two major dimensions – Market Attractiveness and Business Strength. If one of these factors is missing, then the business will not produce desired results. Neither a strong company operating in an unattractive market, nor a weak company operating in an attractive market will do very well.

The vertical axis denotes industry attractiveness, which is a weighted composite rating based on eight different factors. They are:

1. Market size and growth rate
2. Industry profit margins
3. Intensity of Competition
4. Seasonality
5. Product Life Cycle Changes
6. Economies of scale
7. Technology
8. Social, Environmental, Legal and Human Impacts

What does the Horizontal Axis Represent?

It indicates business strength or in other words competitive position, which is again a weighted composite rating based on seven factors as listed below:

1. Relative market share
2. Profit margins
3. Ability to compete on price and quality
4. Knowledge of customer and market
5. Competitive strength and weakness
6. Technological capability
7. Caliber of management

The two composite values for industry attractiveness and competitive position are plotted for each strategic business unit (SBU) in a COMPANY'S PORTFOLIO. The PIE chart (circles) denotes the proportional size of the industry and the dark segments denote the company's respective market share.

The nine cells of the GE matrix are grouped on the basis of low to high industry attractiveness, and weak to strong business strength. Three zones of three cells each are made, indicating different combinations represented by green, yellow and red colors. So it is also called 'Stoplight Strategy Matrix', similar to the traffic signal.

The **invest/grow zone**suggests you to 'go ahead', to grow and build, pushing you through expansion strategies. Businesses in the green zone attract major investment.

Hold/Selective zonecautions you to 'wait and see' indicating hold and maintain type of strategies aimed at stability.

Divest/Harvest zone indicates that you have to adopt turnover strategies of divestment and liquidation or rebuilding approach.

This matrix offers some advantages over BCG matrix in that, it offers intermediate classification of medium and average ratings. It also integrates a larger variety of strategic variables like the market share and industry size.

Advantages

- Helps to prioritize the limited resources in order to achieve the best returns.
- The performance of products or business units becomes evident.
- It's more sophisticated business portfolio framework than the BCG matrix.
- Determines the strategic steps the company needs to adopt to improve the performance of its business portfolio.

Disadvantages

- Needs a consultant or an expert to determine industry's attractiveness and business unit strength as accurately as possible.
- It is expensive to conduct.
- It doesn't take into account the harmony that could exist between two or more business units.

Difference between GE McKinsey and BCG matrices

GE McKinsey matrix is a very similar portfolio evaluation framework to BCG matrix. Both matrices are used to analyze company's product or business unit portfolio and facilitate the investment decisions.

The main differences:

Visual difference. BCG is only a four cell matrix, while GE McKinsey is a nine cell matrix. Nine cells provide better visual portrait of where business units stand in the matrix. It also separates the invest/grow cells from harvest/divest cells that are much closer to each other in the BCG matrix and may confuse others of what investment decisions to make.

- Comprehensiveness. The reason why the GE McKinsey framework was developed is that BCG portfolio tool wasn't sophisticated enough for the guys from General Electric. In BCG matrix, competitive strength of a business unit is equal to relative market share, which assumes that the larger the market share a business has the better it is positioned to compete in the market. This is true, but it's too simplistic to assume that it's the only factor affecting the competition in the market. The same is with industry attractiveness that is measured only as the market growth rate in BCG. It comes to no surprise that GE with its complex business portfolio needed something more comprehensive than that.

Corporate Strategies

Growth is essential for an organization. Organizations go through an inevitable progression from growth through maturity, revival, and eventually decline. The broad corporate strategy alternatives, sometimes referred to as grand strategies, are: stability/consolidation, expansion/growth, divestment/retrenchment and combination strategies. During the organizational life cycle, managements choose between growth, stability, or retrenchment strategies to overcome deteriorating trends in performance.

Just as every product or business unit must follow a business strategy to improve its competitive position, every corporation must decide its orientation towards growth by asking the following three questions:

- Should we expand, cut back, or continue our operations unchanged?
- Should we concentrate our activities within our current industry or should we diversify into other industries?
- If we want to grow and expand nationally and/or globally, should we do so through internal development or through external acquisitions, mergers, or strategic alliances?

At the core of corporate strategy must be a clear logic of how the corporate objectives, will be achieved. Most of the strategic choices of successful corporations have a central economic logic that serves as the fulcrum for profit creation. Some of the major economic reasons for choosing a particular type corporate strategy are:

a. Exploiting operational economies and financial economies of scope.
b. Uncertainty avoidance and efficiency.
c. Possession of management skills that help create corporate advantage.
d. Overcoming the inefficiency in factor markets and
e. Long term profit potential of a business.

The non-economic reasons for the choice of corporate strategy elements include :

a. Dominant view of the top management,
b. Employee incentives to diversify (maximizing management compensation),
c. Desire for more power and management control,
d. Ethical considerations and e) corporate social responsibility.

There are four types of generic **corporate strategies**. They are:

- Stability strategies: make no change to the company's current activities
- Growth strategies: expand the company's activities
- Retrenchment strategies: reduce the company's level of activities
- Combination strategies: a combination of above strategies

Each one of the above strategies has a specific objective. For instance, a concentration strategy seeks to increase the growth of a single product line while a diversification strategy seeks to alter a firm's strategic track by adding new product lines. A stability strategy is utilized by a firm to achieve steady, but slow improvements in growth while a retrenchment strategy (which includes harvesting, turnaround, divestiture, or liquidation strategies) is used to reverse poor-organizational performance. Once a strategic direction has been identified, it then becomes necessary for management to examine business and functional level strategies of the firm to make sure that all units are moving towards the achievement of the company-wide corporate strategy.

Corporate Strategies

Stability Strategy

Stability strategy is a strategy in which the organization retains its present strategy at the corporate level and continues focusing on its present products and markets. The firm stays with its current business and product markets; maintains the existing level of effort; and is satisfied with incremental growth. It does not seek to invest in new factories and capital assets, gain market share, or invade new geographical territories. Organizations choose this strategy when the industry in which it operates or the state of the economy is in turmoil or when the industry faces slow or no growth prospects. They also choose this strategy when they go through a period of rapid expansion and need to consolidate their operations before going for another bout of expansion.

Expansion or Growth Strategy

Firms choose expansion strategy when their perceptions of resource availability and past financial performance are both high. The most common growth strategies are diversification at the corporate level and concentration at the business level. Reliance Industry, a vertically integrated company covering the complete textile value chain has been repositioning itself to be a diversified conglomerate by entering into a range of business such as power generation and distribution, insurance, telecommunication, and information and communication technology services. Diversification is defined as the entry of a firm into new lines of activity, through internal or external modes. The primary reason a firm pursues increased diversification are value creation through economies of scale and scope, or market dominance. In some cases firms choose diversification because of government policy, performance problems and uncertainty about future cash flow. In one sense, diversification is a risk management tool, in that its successful use reduces a firm's vulnerability to the consequences of competing in a single market or industry. Risk plays a very vital role in selecting a strategy and hence, continuous evaluation of risk is linked with a firm's ability to achieve strategic advantage (Simons, 1999). Internal development can take the form of investments in new products, services, customer segments, or geographic markets including international expansion. Diversification is accomplished through external modes through acquisitions and joint ventures. Concentration can be achieved through vertical or horizontal growth. Vertical growth occurs when a firm takes over a function previously provided by a supplier or a distributor. Horizontal growth occurs when the firm expands products into new geographic areas or increases the range of products and services in current markets.

Retrenchment Strategy

Many firms experience deteriorating financial performance resulting from market erosion and wrong decisions by management. Managers respond by selecting corporate strategies that redirect their attempt to turnaround the company by improving their firm's competitive position or divest or wind up the business if a turnaround is not possible. Turnaround strategy is a form of retrenchment strategy, which focuses on operational improvement when the state of decline is not severe. Other possible corporate level strategic responses to decline include growth and stability.

Combination Strategy

The three generic strategies can be used in combination; they can be sequenced, for instance growth followed by stability, or pursued simultaneously in different parts of the business unit. Combination Strategy is designed to mix growth, retrenchment, and stability strategies and apply them across a corporation's business units. A firm adopting the combination strategy may apply the combination either simultaneously (across the different businesses) or sequentially. For instance, Tata Iron & Steel Company (TISCO) had first consolidated its position in the core steel business, then divested some of its non-core businesses. Reliance Industries, while consolidating its position in the existing businesses such as textile and petrochemicals, aggressively entered new areas such as Information Technology.

3.5.   Balanced Score Card

The Balanced Scorecard (BSC) is a business framework used for tracking and managing an organization's strategy.

The BSC framework is based on the balance between leading and lagging indicators, which can respectively be thought of as the *drivers* and *outcomes* of your company goals. When used in the Balanced Scorecard framework, these key indicators tell you whether or not you're accomplishing your goals and whether you're on the right track to accomplish future goals.

With a Balanced Scorecard, you have the capability to:

- Describe your strategy.
- Measure your strategy.
- Track the actions you're taking to improve upon your results.

Uses of Balanced score card:

A Balanced Scorecard is most often used in three ways:

1. **To bring an organization's strategy to life.** Those in the company can then use this strategy to make decisions company-wide.
2. **To communicate the strategy across the organization.** This is where the strategy map is critical. Organizations print it and include it in interoffice communications, put it on their intranet, communicate it with business partners, publish it on their website, and more.
3. **To track strategic performance.** That's typically done through monthly, quarterly, and annual reports.

3.6. Life Cycle Analysis

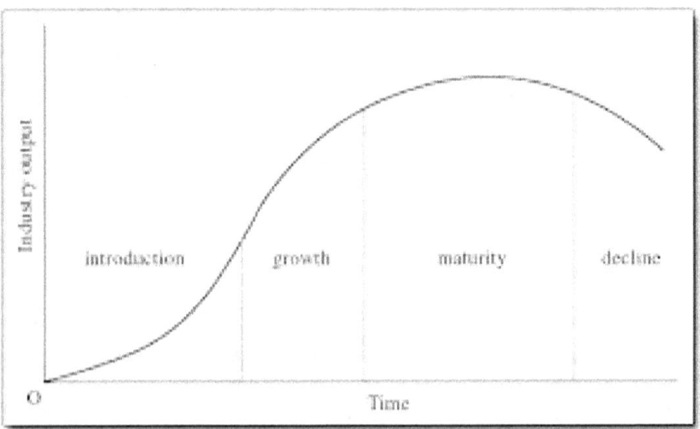

The life cycle is basic to understanding the significance the portfolio approaches. The concept has been around for so long and is so widely used that it is difficult to trace its originator.

The product/service life cycle holds that products and markets and entire industries develop, grow rapidly, mature, saturate, and decline in a somewhat predictable fashion. If sales are plotted as a function of time, this predictable pattern is a lazy-*S* *curve*. The traditional stages in an industry's life cycle are shown in the above figure.

In the **introduction** phase, the output industry (products or services) is initially offered to the customers, and sales are slowly built up as more customers become aware of product. At this stage in the industry's development, choice of technology is often not yet settled.

After a certain critical mass of demand has been established, sales take off in an exponential growth rate as increasingly large numbers of new customers demand the product for the first time, the industry enters the **growth stage.**

At this stage, most buyers are still first-time purchasers of the industry's outputs. Over time, growth of the industry begins to slow as marked demand approaches saturation. Fewer first-time buyers remain; most purchase are now for replacement purposes. When the market demand for the industry/s outputs is completely saturated, the **maturity** stage has been reached.

As technology makes the product obsolete, or as substitute products arrive, sales decline. This **decline** stage is often ushered in when consumers begin to turn to the products or services of substitute industries.

There are problems with using the Life Cycle Concept as a precise strategic decision making tool. It is almost impossible to predict how long a certain phase of the life cycle will last or know the height of the curve (unit sold). Thus, the concept's use as a forecasting tool is very limited.

CHAPTER IV

STRATEGIC FORMULATION AND IMPLEMENTATION

4.1. Strategic Implementation

The activity performed according to a plan in order to achieve an overall goal. For example, strategic implementation within a business context might involve developing and then executing a new marketing plan to help increase sales of the company's products to consumers.

Steps in Implementing a Strategy

1. Developing an organization having potential of carrying out strategy successfully.
2. Disbursement of abundant resources to strategy-essential activities.
3. Creating strategy-encouraging policies.
4. Employing best policies and programs for constant improvement.
5. Linking reward structure to accomplishment of results.
6. Making use of strategic leadership.

Excellently formulated strategies will fail if they are not properly implemented. Also, it is essential to note that strategy implementation is not possible unless there is stability between strategy and each organizational dimension such as organizational structure, reward structure, resource-allocation process, etc.

Strategy implementation poses a threat to many managers and employees in an organization. New power relationships are predicted and achieved. New groups (formal as well as informal) are formed whose values, attitudes, beliefs and concerns may not be known. With the change in power and status roles, the managers and employees may employ confrontation behavior.

Avoiding the Implementation Pitfalls

If you want your plan to succeed, heed the advice here and stay away from the pitfalls of implementing your strategic plan. Here are the most common reasons strategic plans fail:

1. Lack of Ownership

The most common reason a plan fails is lack of ownership. If people don't have a stake and responsibility in the plan, it'll be business as usual for all but a frustrated few.

2. Lack of Communication

The plan doesn't get communicated to employees, and they don't understand how they contribute.

3. Getting Mired in the Day-to-day

Owners and managers, consumed by daily operating problems, lose sight of long-term goals. Out of the ordinary: The plan is treated as something separate and removed from the management process.

4. An Overwhelming Plan

The goals and actions generated in the strategic planning session are too numerous because the team failed to make tough choices to eliminate non-critical actions. Employees don't know where to begin.

5. A Meaningless Plan

The vision, mission, and value statements are viewed as fluff and not supported by actions or don't have employee buy-in.

6. Annual Strategy

Strategy is only discussed at yearly weekend retreats. Not considering implementation: Implementation isn't discussed in the strategic planning process. The planning document is seen as an end in itself.

7. No Progress Report

There's no method to track progress, and the plan only measures what's easy, not what's important. No one feels any forward momentum.

8. No Accountability

Accountability and high visibility help drive change. This means that each measure, objective, data source, and initiative must have an owner.

9. Lack of Empowerment

Although accountability may provide strong motivation for improving performance, employees must also have the authority, responsibility, and tools necessary to impact relevant measures. Otherwise, they may resist involvement and ownership. It's easier to avoid pitfalls when they're clearly identified.

Barriers to STRATEGY Implementation

Listed below are the top four barriers they selected, providing tips to eliminate them so your credit union's strategy will be easier to implement.

1. Lack of Inspiration and Motivation from Senior Management

Simply put, senior management has to demonstrate they are passionate about the business and encourage others to feel that same kind of passion. They have to connect with their employees in other ways, too: listening to their employees, including them in the decisions they make, demonstrating integrity and giving people what they want within the executive's capability – i.e. if not money, then verbal recognition, or some other demonstration of appreciation for good work.

2. No Clear Communications

Communication is about the creation of meaning and understanding, not simply moving information around. Senior managers need to dialog regularly with employees about the organization's purpose, goals, projects, differentiation, members, competitors, and how their departments and the employee's personal efforts contribute to the organization. It's about clarity – it's about inspecting what you expect. Repetition is a good thing – even if the executives themselves may be bored with the subject matter. Former General Electric chief and author Jack Welch said that it took him six years of constantly telling his employees, *you are first or second in your business or you are out,* before they really understood (believed) it.

3. Inconsistency among Management about what to do and how to do it

Standards are essential for any company that seeks to improve. Continuous improvement methods are based on a repeatable process – and employees leverage their learning from participating in the process. A stable process is a framework for collecting, and evaluating, performance. Once you are collecting performance information on the process, you have a platform to develop improvement opportunities. Consider the following two scenarios: When you are driving a car, you can be driving 50 miles an hour (or more) and you can predict that the other drivers barreling down the freeway will follow the "rules of the road." Drivers have adopted a standard that is predictable to any other driver on the road – which makes driving FAST very productive – and relatively safe.

However, anyone who owns a boat knows that a boat owner cannot rely on any other boat operators to behave according to waterways rules (or standards for operating a boat). Consequently, when you are speeding across the lake, assume there is another boat barreling down to cross your bow from the left. According to rules of the waterways, you have the right of way. The other boat is supposed to slow down and let you pass across his bow (allowing you to continue at your current speed).

Lacking standards, or lacking the organizational discipline to ensure everyone complies with the work standards you have, really slows down your organization. No one can afford to slow down, so be sure to review what standards your organization has in place and ask yourself this question: Is your organization disciplined enough to comply with those standards and use the learning to improve those standard processes? One other big benefit to standardizing the process is it reduces inconsistency among management about what to do and how to do it – reducing stress and wasted effort among management's employees.

4. We Alreadyhave too much to do – and not enough time to do it

According to a recent Accenture study, the average middle manager is swamped by useless information and spends about two hours a day looking for the data he or she needs. Once the information is found, Accenture reports that half the information has no value to their jobs. Companies tend to have "silos" of information, each department having its own system for organizing data – structured or unstructured. This information is not shared or access is difficult by other people outside the "silo" who could benefit from it. At least annually, managers should conduct a communication audit of meetings and reports and eliminate certain meetings and reports that are not useful. Develop and implement standard systems for organizing data, making sure that access to information across the enterprise encourages organizational transparency.

The Importance of Strategic Implementation

1. Function

Without strategic implementation, a project would not be able to get off the ground, since strategic implementation functions as a project's blueprint. The implementation process identifies what tasks need to be completed, and when. Strategic implementation is action-based and uses a variety of tools to keep the project team on track.

2. Work Breakdown Structure

A work breakdown structure is an asset to any project team because it illustrates the order of operations for project implementation. Work breakdown structures identify all the steps that need to be taken to get from one implementation phase to the next. According to Net MBA, work breakdown structures are designed in a hierarchal structure, and break a project down into smaller, and more manageable, components.

3. Implementation Schedule

Another valuable application that strategic implementation is responsible for is developing an implementation schedule. Implementation schedules are similar to time lines in that they dictate start and end dates for when project tasks and phases should be completed. According to the U.S. Army Corps of Engineers, project implementation schedules are often broken down into charts that map out the duration of how long a task should be performed before it's on to the next phase.

4. Cost Allocation

Strategic implementation is important because it evaluates project costs and determines cost allocation to fund the project from start to finish. By planning ahead, and conducting financial studies and projections, the strategic implementation process can save projects money in the end, because unforeseen costs can be reduced or eliminated.

5. Evaluation Methodology

The strategic implementation process will determine the evaluation methodology for a project. Evaluations are done to study how close a project is to being completed, and if the project team has met important milestones. Evaluations consist of measuring a project's progress, and comparing that against what the targeted goal is. This will tell the project team whether or not they are on track with the projected time frames and projected funding.

Characteristics of Strategic Decisions

1. Future Orientation

Long-term future direction of the organization is an important aspect of strategic decisions. Strategic decisions often emerge from the perspective views about the company and society, including regulatory environment, prospects of different business, industry structure, competitive environment, etc.

2. Value Orientation

As it is implicit in the point mentioned above, strategic decisions are affected by the value system, including business ethics and philosophy.

3. Scope of the Organization

The long term direction and value orientation influence the definition of the scope of the activities of the organization. The business/businesses the organization should be in is key decision in strategic management.

4. Means to End

Strategy is the means to achieve the end, i.e., the mission and goals.

5. Resource Commitment

Strategic decisions being long term in nature and having to do with the scope of the business of the organization may imply major resource commitments, including reallocation of existing resources.

6. Strategic Fit

Strategic decisions seek to establish a sustainable organization environment fit. The quintessence of strategic management is the effective deployment of organizational resources or strengths to exploit the environmental opportunities and to combat the environmental threats.

7. Intent and Stretch

Strategy is also viewed as a stretch emanating from strategic intent.

8. Competitive Orientation

Strategic decisions aim at gaining a sustainable competitive edge of the firm.

9. Ramifications

Strategic decisions may affect operational and administrative decision.

10. Complexity

As strategic decisions encompasses mission, long-term direction, scope of the organization, and establishment of organization environment fit, they are often complex in nature.

11. Uncertainty

Because of the long term future perspective of the strategic decisions, they can involve considerable uncertainty as future can hardly be predicted exactly.

12. Comprehensive and Integrated

A strategy is normally comprehensive and highly integrated.

Process of Strategy Implementation

1. Align your Initiatives

A key road to failed implementation is when we create a new strategy but then continue to do the same things of old. A new strategy means new priorities and new activities across the organization. Every activity (other than the most functional) must be reviewed against its relevance to the new strategy. A good way of doing this is to create a strategic value measurement tool for existing and new initiatives. Initiatives should be analyzed against their strategic value and the impact to the organization.

2. Align Budgets &Performance

Ideally your capital budgets are decentralized, so each division can both allocate and manage the budgets to deliver the division's strategic initiatives. Norton and Kaplan in their recent book 'The Execution Premium' recommend cross functional strategic initiatives be allocated specific budget (STRATEX) alongside capital (CAPEX) and operating (OPEX) budgets. This protects strategic expenditure from being re-allocated to short-term requirements of OPEX whilst subjecting strategic initiatives to a rigorous review (eg. forecasted revenue growth and productivity) much like is done for CAPEX.

Organizational performance should be closely aligned to strategy. Performance measures should be placed against strategic goals across the organization and each division and staff member. All staff will have job functions that will impact on strategy. Most staff will have impact across a series of strategic goals (eg. financial, customer service, product). Ensure employees are aware of their role and influence on strategy delivery and performance. This is also important to employee engagement (see below).

3. Structure Follows Strategy

A transformational strategy may require a transformation to structure. Does the structure of your organization allow strategy to cascade across and down the organization in a way that meaningfully and efficiently delivers the strategy. Organizations that try and force a new strategy into an out-dated structure will find their strategy implementation eventually reaches a deadlock.

4. Engaging Staff

The key reason strategy execution fails is because the organization doesn't get behind it. If you're staff and critical stakeholders don't understand the strategy and fail to engage, then the strategy has failed. The importance of this step cannot be understated. If you're staff are not delivering the strategy, then the strategy has failed.

4.1. Prepare

Strategy involves change. Change is difficult and human tendency is to resist it. So not matter how enlightened and inspiring your new strategic vision, it will come up against hurdles. Tipping Point Leadership theory (a key principle of the Blue Ocean Strategy methodology) outlines four key hurdles that executives must overcome to achieve execution. Those hurdles are cognitive, resource, motivation and political hurdles. It is important we understand each of these hurdles and develop strategies to overcome them.

4.2. Include

Bring influential employees, not just executive team members into the planning process. Not only will they contribute meaningfully to strategy, they will also be critical in ensuring the organization engages with the strategy. Furthermore, listen across the organization during strategy formulation. Some of your best ideas will come from within your organization, not the executive team (think 3M's Post-It Notes)

4.3. Communicate

Ensure every staff member understands the strategic vision, the strategic themes and what their role will be in delivering the strategic vision. And enrich the communication experience. Communicate the strategy through a combination of presentations, workshops, meetings, newsletters, intranets and updates. Continue strategy and performance updates throughout the year.

4.4. Clarify

It is important that all employees are aware of expectations. How are they expected to change? What and how are they expected to deliver? Each individual must understand their functions within the strategy, the expected outcomes and how they will be measured. As mentioned above performance measures and incentives should be aligned with performance against strategic KPIs.

5. Monitor and Adapt

A strategy must be a living, breathing document. As we all know: if there's one constant in business these days it's change. So our strategies must be adaptable and flexible so they can respond to changes in both our internal and external environments. Strategy meetings should be held regularly throughout the year, where initiatives and direction are assessed for performance and strategic relevance. At least once a year we should put our strategy under full review to check it against changes in our external and competitive environments as well as our internal environments.

Strategy is not just a document written by executive teams and filed in the CEO's desk. It is a vision for the organisation, owned by the organisation. And to succeed the whole organisation must engage with it and live and breathe it. Strategy should inform our operations, our structure, and how we go about doing what we do. It should be the pillar against which we assess our priorities, our actions and performance. When execution is brought into strategic planning we find that our strategy is weaved through our organisation, and it's from here that great leaps in growth and productivity can be achieved.

4.2. Functions of Top Level Management

The main functions of top level management are as follows:

1. Determine Objectives for the Organisation

Objectives may relate to profit, business growth, survival, prestige, competitive pricing, marketing method, widening the area of sales, relations with workers, customers, public etc.

2. Frame the Policy

To frame the policy and chalk out the plans to carry out the objectives and policies may relate to different aspects of the organisation. For example, production policy deals with the quality, product variety, scheduling of production to meet the market demand etc.

3. Market Policy

This policy deals with such matters as advertising and sales promotion techniques, pricing product, channel of distribution, commission, discount, placements, training, remuneration promotion, appraisal of performance etc. of the personnel.

4. Financial Policy

This relates to the procurement of funds, source of finance, management of earning, etc.

5. Organisational Frame Work

Top management determines the organizational structure for the purpose of executing the plans that have been laid down. Execution of plans is necessary to carry out the objectives and policies.

6. Assemble the Resources

For the purpose of executing the plans, the resources of men, machines, materials and money have to be assembled. This again is the task of top management.

7. Control the Operations through Organisation

Controls the top management regarding operations through budgets, cost and statistics quality control and accounting devices

4.3. Role of the CEO and Management

1. Operating the Corporation

The CEO and management run the corporation's day-to-day business operations. With a thorough understanding of how the corporation operates and earns its income, they carry out the corporation's strategic objectives within the annual operating plans and budgets, which the board reviews. In making decisions about the corporation's business operations, the CEO considers the long-term interests of the corporation and its shareholders and necessarily relies on the input and advice of others, including the board, senior management and outside advisers. The CEO keeps the board apprised of significant developments regarding the corporation's business operations.

2. Strategic Planning

The CEO and senior management generally take the lead in strategic planning. They identify and develop strategic plans designed to create long-term value for the corporation, present those plans to the board, implement the plans once board review is completed, and recommend and carry out changes to the plans as necessary. As part of the strategic planning process, the CEO and senior management identify, evaluate and manage risks associated with the plans.

3. Identifying, Evaluating and Managing Risks

Management identifies, evaluates and manages the risks that the corporation undertakes in implementing its strategic plans and in the course of carrying out its business. It also manages the corporation's overall risk profile, and senior management keeps the board informed on an ongoing basis about the corporation's significant risks and its risk management processes.

4. Annual Operating Plans and Budgets

With the corporation's overall strategic plans in mind, senior management develops annual operating plans and budgets for the corporation and presents the plans and budgets to the board. Once the board has reviewed the annual operating plans and budgets, the management team implements them and monitors them, making changes as appropriate in light of changing conditions, assumptions or expectations. The management team also keeps the board apprised of significant developments and changes relating to the annual operating plans and budgets.

5. Selecting Qualified Management and Establishing an Effective Organizational Structure

Senior management is responsible for selecting qualified management and implementing an organizational structure that is efficient and appropriate for the corporation's particular circumstances.

6. Accurate and Transparent Financial Reporting and Disclosures

Management is responsible for the integrity of the corporation's financial reporting system, and the accurate and timely preparation of the corporation's financial statements and related disclosures in accordance with Generally Accepted Accounting Principles and in compliance with applicable laws and regulations. It is management's responsibility—under the direction of the CEO and the corporation's principal financial officer—to establish, maintain and periodically evaluate the corporation's internal controls over financial reporting and the corporation's disclosure controls and procedures. In accordance with applicable law and regulations, the CEO and the corporation's principal financial officer also are responsible for certifying the accuracy and completeness of the corporation's financial statements and the effectiveness of the corporation's internal and disclosure controls.

The CEO and management are responsible for operating the corporation in an ethical manner. They should never put individual, personal interests before those of the corporation or its shareholders. Business Roundtable believes that when carrying out this function, corporations should have:

7. A CEO of Integrity

The CEO should be a person of integrity who takes responsibility for the corporation adhering to the highest ethical standards.

8. A strong, Ethical "tone at the top."

The CEO and senior management should set a "tone at the top" that establishes a culture of legal compliance and integrity communicated to personnel at all levels of the corporation.

9. An Effective Compliance Program

Management should take responsibility for implementing and managing an effective compliance program and should report regularly to the board on compliance matters. As part of its compliance program, a corporation should have a code of conduct with effective reporting and enforcement mechanisms. Employees should have a means of seeking guidance and alerting management and the board about potential or actual misconduct without fear of retribution, and violations of the code should be addressed promptly and effectively.

4.4.   Matching Structure Strategy

Step 1Review the different organizational structures most commonly used. Understand that a functional structure organizes workers by the job performed, a divisional structure is organized by product or service produced, and a matrix structure is a combination of the two.

Step 2 Review your business size. Because few businesses that employ less than 12 to 15 employees have the manpower to implement the divisional or matrix structure, it is likely that a firm of this size will need to implement a functional structure. Recognize, however, if you intend your company to grow rapidly and recruit heavily that you may begin with a functional structure and plan for an evolution into one of the other structures as they become more appropriate.

Step 3 Analyze the organizational structures of your competitors. See if there are any variations in the structures they use and if those differences attribute to comparable business success. Research each company's history to see if there have been any deviations from their current structure, and what were the reasons and the impacts of the changes in structure.

Step 4 Identify the standard structure used throughout your industry. See if there are any significant reasons why that structure is the best for your particular product or service. Recognize, for example, if the markets your industry serves are typically located in different regions, then a divisional structure may be more appropriate than any other. Identify how your industry typically locates its work groups, such as an import businesses based at international ports. This could indicate whether your business type can support a decentralized divisional structure or a more centralized functional one.

Step 5 Review the costs of maintaining the different organizational structures. Maintaining a divisional structure requires that each division operates as an independent business unit and cost center resulting in higher operational costs compared to a centralized functional structure. Recognize that the matrix structure creates redundancies by incorporating elements of both functional and divisional structures, so operational costs are even higher than the other two.

Step 6 Weigh the benefits that each structure can bring to your organization. Know that although the divisional structure offers more flexibility than the functional structure, it does not offer the level of operational control, and the matrix offers the benefits of both. Identify if the implementation of one of the three structures will offer any significant advantage that will make your company more competitive in the market.

4.5.   Resource Allocation

Resource allocation is used to assign the available resources in an economic way. It is part of resource management. In project management, resource allocation is the scheduling of activities and the resources required by those activities while taking into consideration both the resource availability and the project time.

Resource Allocation

In strategic planning, a resource-allocation decision is a plan for using available resources, especially human resources especially in the near term, to achieve goals for the future. It is the process of allocating resources among the various projects or business units. **The plan has two parts:**

Firstly, there is the basic allocation decision and secondly there are contingency mechanisms. The basic allocation decision is the choice of which items to fund in the plan, and what level of funding it should receive, and which to leave unfunded: the resources are allocated to some items, not to others.

There are two contingency mechanisms. There is a priority ranking of items excluded from the plan, showing which items to fund if more resources should become available; and there is a priority ranking of some items included in the plan, showing which items should be sacrificed if total funding must be reduced. Resource allocation is a major management activity that allows for strategy execution. In organizations that do not use a strategic-management approach to decision making, resource allocation is often based on political or personal factors. Strategic management enables resources to be allocated according to priorities established by annual objectives. Nothing could be more detrimental to strategic management and to organizational success than for resources to be allocated in ways not consistent with priorities indicated by approved annual objectives.

All organizations have at least four types of resources that can be used to achieve desired objectives:

Financial resources, physical resources, human resources, and technological resources. Allocating resources to particular divisions and departments does not mean that strategies will be successfully implemented. A number of factors commonly prohibit effective resource allocation, including an overprotection of resources, too great an emphasis on short-run financial criteria, organizational politics, vague strategy targets, a reluctance to take risks, and a lack of sufficient knowledge. Managers normally have many more tasks than they can do. Managers must allocate time and resources among these tasks. Pressure builds up. Expenses are too high. The CEO wants a good financial report for the third quarter. Strategy formulation and implementation activities often get deferred. Today's problems soak up available energies and resources. Scrambled accounts and budgets fail to reveal the shift in allocation away from strategic needs to currently squeaking wheels. The real value of any resource allocation program lies in the resulting accomplishment of an organization's objectives. Effective resource allocation does not guarantee successful strategy implementation because programs, personnel, controls, and commitment must breathe life into the resources provided. Strategic management itself is sometimes referred to as a "resource allocation process."

The Following Factors Affect Resource Allocation

1. **Objectives: Resource** allocation must be oriented to objectives achievement. Objectives should be clearly laid down with strategic priorities for resource allocation. Critical success factors are considered.
2. **Managerial preferences:** Top managers who are dominated in strategy formulation tend t affect resources allocation. Their preferences attract more resources for their pet projects.
3. **Internal policies: Resources** area a symbol of power. Internal policies based on negotiations and bargaining affects resources allocation.
4. **External influences: The** demands of stakeholders also affect resource allocation. They can be owners, suppliers, customers, employees, bankers and community. Legal requirements may require additional resources allocation. For example pollution control, safety and labour welfare requirement.

Types of Resource Allocation

We can begin by defining resource allocation. In a broad sense, it can be defined as how things can be distributed. This may include credit, blame, responsibility, money, time, and the like. In the science and engineering this translates to: money, consumables, time, space, and services. Naturally there needs to be a "fair" way to distribute these resources. This section outlines way to distribute these resources.

Allocation by Merit

- This can be seen as a rewards system of sorts. This view suggests that rewards should be distributed according to productivity, effort, or demonstrated ability.
- In the work place, this can be seen as salary increases, promotions, and even layoffs.

- In the college environment, this can be seen as the distribution of grades. As not everyone can receive an A for classes, the grades need to be distributed reflecting a students understanding of the subject.
- In aspects where a necessity is involved, such as food, shelter, and water, this system breaks down. In impoverished countries, for example, few would argue for denying children food because they are not as productive as adults.

Allocation by Social Worth

- Allocation by social worth tends to take a practical view toward resources, directing them toward those who appear most likely to contribute to the common good. This view suggests that resources should move in directions that ultimately do the greatest good for the largest number of people. Criteria for social worth can include age, seniority, rank, and expertise.
- In the work place, this can be seen as layoffs. Generally speaking, a senior worker will not be fired over a new worker.
- In the college environment, this can be seen as the distribution of money to labs. Labs for graduate students and upperclassmen tend to be better than freshman labs.
- Allocation by social worth breaks down when the criteria for worth ignores basic human rights. For example, wealth is sometimes used to measure social worth, especially in countries with market economies. This attitude can cause food, energy, education, medical attention, and social influence to "flow uphill," thereby making severe imbalances in essential resources even worse.

Allocation by Need

- Allocation by need tends to view resources in terms of basic human rights. This view suggests that every person has the same right to some minimal level of a given resource. Obvious examples include food, shelter, and clothes.
- In the work place, this can be seen when a company diverts funds to a division in that company who's equipment is outdated.
- In the college environment, this can be seen as scholarships given to students who otherwise would not be able to attend college.
- Allocation by need breaks down when this criterion is applied so strictly that it removes the incentive to produce. It's usually true that people work hardest when they believe they will enjoy the fruits of their labors. This is also the same reason why socialism doesn't work.

Allocation by Equal or Random Assignment

- Allocation by equal or random assignment takes the view that no rational, unbiased way can be found to distribute resources. This is the default allocation method when no other allocation method works.
- The most obvious example of this is a lottery. When there is no obvious way to distribute resources, a simple lottery can prove to be the "fairest" way.
- Allocation by random assignment breaks down when each portion of a resource is simply too small to do any good. For example, dividing antibiotics into small doses during an epidemic could make each dose so small that no one benefits.

Strategic Controls

Strategic controls are used to evaluate the overall performance of an organization or a significant component of that performance. In the private sector, standards such as profitability, ratio of assets to liabilities, sales growth, and return on investment provide a broad basis on which to assess the overall performance of an organization. In recent years, standards applicable to public sector activities have been detailed in terms of measures of effectiveness. When organizations fail to meet such broad strategic control standards, the remedies may need to be equally broad. They may include the recasting of goals and objectives, reformulating plans and programs, changes in organizational structure, improved internal and external communications, and so on. Strategic controls should assist decision makers in identifying when unanticipated changes occur in the broader environment and in determining appropriate corrective actions. In addition to monitoring the results of past decisions (through financial measures), strategic controls should include measures of the organization's ability to build competitive advantages in terms of efficiency, quality of service, innovation, and responsiveness to customers (measures of future performance). As Hill and Jones observed, Strategic control is not just monitoring how well an organization and its members are achieving current goals or about how well the firm is utilizing its existing resources. It is also about keeping employees motivated, focused on the important problems confronting an organization now and in the future, and working together to find solutions that can help an organization perform better over time.

A system of strategic controls should provide a basis by which goals and objectives can be modified and the methods of control can be enhanced to achieve increased productivity and overall effectiveness.

Specifications for Controls

1. Control is a principle of economy. The fewer the controls, the more effective they will be. Adding more controls does not give better control. All it does is create confusion.

2. Controls must be meaningful. Events to be measured must be significant either in themselves or must be symptoms of at least potentially significant developments. Controls should always be related to key objectives and priorities.

3. Controls must be appropriate to the character and nature of the phenomena measured. The measures selected must have formal validity and statistical reliability. But more importantly, they must be measuring the right things.

4. Measurements must be congruent with the events measured. It is important to avoid the trap of false precision: to know when an approximation is more accurate than a precise-looking figure worked out in great detail. Qualitative descriptions of phenomena often are more accurate (and more rigorous) than any specific figures.

5. Controls must be timely. The time dimension of controls should correspond to the time span of the event being measured. Frequent measurement and rapid "feedback" do not necessarily give better control. "Real time" often is the wrong time span for real control.

6. Controls need to be simple. Complicated controls tend to confuse and to misdirect attention from what is to be controlled toward the mechanics and methods of control. Controls that are overly complex and contain ambiguities and subtleties seldom work.

7. Controls must be operational. Controls must focus on action and must fall within the realm of responsibility of those individuals who are capable of taking the controlling action.

CHAPTER V

STRATEGIC EVALUATION AND CONTROL

5.1. Strategic Evaluation and Control

Introduction

Strategic Evaluation is defined as the process of determining the effectiveness of a given strategy in achieving the organizational objectives and taking corrective action wherever required. Strategic evaluation and control is related to that aspect of strategic management through which an organisation ensures whether it is achieving its objectives Contemplated in the strategic action.

Definition

Glueck and Jauch have defined strategic evaluation as follows: "Evaluation of strategy is that phase of the strategic management process in which the top managers determine whether their strategic choice as implemented is meeting the objectives of the enterprise".

There are two aspects in this phase of strategic management: evaluation which emphasizes measurement of results of a strategic action and control which emphasizes on taking necessary actions in the light of gap that exists between intended results and actual results in the strategic action. However, because of on-going nature of strategic evaluation and control process.both these are intertwined. In practice. The term control is used in a broad sense which includes evaluative aspect too because unless the results of an action are known, control actions cannot be taken.

5.2. Importance of Strategic Evaluation and Control

They provide direction. They enable management to make sure that the organisation is heading in the right direction and that corrective action is taken where needed.

They provide guidance to everybody. Everyone within the organisation, both managers and workers alike, learn what is happening, how their performance compares with what is expected, and what needs to be done to keep up the good work or improve performance.

They inspire confidence. Information about good performance inspires confidence in everybody. Those within the organisation are likely to be more motivated to maintain and achieve better performance in order to keep up their track record. Those outside – customers, government authorities, shareholders – are likely to be impressed with the good performance.

5.3.   Evaluation and Control Criteria

In putting the control process in operation, two basic issues are involved what to control and how to control. The first issue is related, to the identification of those factors on the basis of which degree of business success is determined. The second issue involves the use of various control techniques.

Criteria of Business Success

The success of any organisation, whether business or nonbusiness.Measured in terms of its objective achievement. Since an organisation May pursue a number of objectives simultaneously, and these may be expressed: in different forms. There are a number of criteria which are used for control. These criteria are grouped into two categories: intervening criteria and end-result criteria as shown in Figure.

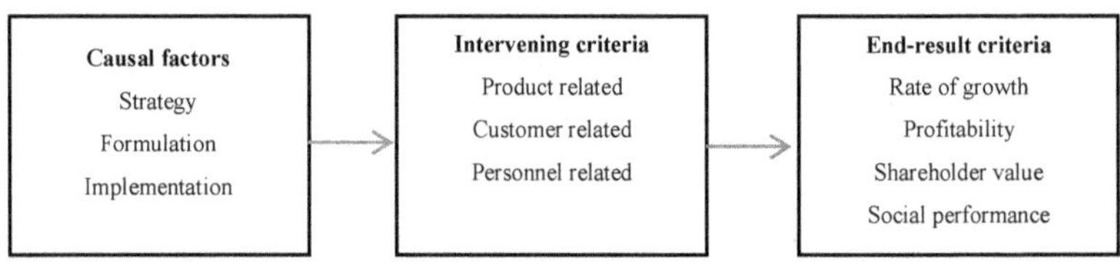

Evaluation and Control Criteria

Causal Factors

Causal factors are those that influence the course of development in an organisation. These are independent variables and affect intervening criteria and through these, end-result criteria. For example, strategy formulation and its implementation affects various product, customer, and personnel related criteria. These, in turn, affect different end-result criteria which are used, generally, to measure business performance.

Intervening Criteria

Intervening criteria are those factors which are reflected as the internal state of the organisation. These are caused by causal factors and, therefore, cannot be changed independently except by changing causal factors; in this case type of strategy and its implementation. For example, personnel attitudes and morale, an intervening criterion, cannot be changed unless there is a suitable change in organisational design, systems, and leadership-all being elements of strategy implementation. Intervening criteria are, generally grouped into three categories: product, customer, and personnel related. An illustrative list of intervening criteria is given below:

Product Related Criteria

- Product quality and performance
- Product cost and price
- New products introduced

Customer Related Criteria

- Customer service
- Customer satisfaction
- Customer loyalty

Personnel Related Criteria

- Attracting and retaining human talent
- Personnel ability and skills
- Personnel motivation and attitudes to work

End-result Criteria

End-result criteria are those factors which are caused by causal and intervening factors and are often in terms of the criteria in which organizational success is measured. These factors are highly dependent and, therefore, cannot be changed except by changing the factors responsible for these. End-result criteria are grouped in four categories: rate of growth, profitability, shareholder value, and social performance. Given below is the illustrative list of these factors:

Rate of Growth

- Sales growth
- Market share
- Asset increase

Profitability

- Profit-sales relationship
- Return on value added
- Return on investment

Shareholder Value

- Dividend payment
- Bonus shares
- Market price of shares

Social Performance

Satisfaction of various stakeholders. After identifying the factors to be evaluated, another issue comes in the form of fixing standard in respect of these factors. Since many factors are in qualitative form and others are in quantitative form, both qualitative and quantitative standard are set for evaluation and control. At this stage, it will be worthwhile to understand the criteria that are used by companies for strategic evaluation and control. Table presents the findings of a study of 72 companies on the criteria used by these companies.

Factors for Strategic Evaluation and Control

Factor	Average
1. Value added	2.32
2. Return on value added	1.56
3. ROV A/ROI	2.21
4. Attracting and retaining talent	2.25
5. Number of future managers Developed	2.06
6. New product development	2.20
7. Improved service to customers	2.65
8. Competitive return to shareholders	2.25
9. Maximisation of shareholders' value	2.14

Measured at 4-point Scale

The above study shows the various factors for strategic evaluation and control in general form. Let us take the case of factors used for measuring a company's performance. *Financial Express,* a daily financial newspaper, uses the following criteria for selecting the best company of the year as shown in Exhibit

Exhibit

Criteria for Performance Measurement Used by Financial Express

1. Export revenue for competitiveness
2. Cash plough back/total debt for capability to reduce debt
3. Profit after tax/net worth for profitability
4. Plough back to net worth for capability to use internal accruals
5. Interest cover for ability to serve lenders
6. Gross profit/sales for profit margin

7. Earnings before depreciation, interest and tax/total assets for ability to use assets

8. Profit after tax/assets for profitability in using assets

9. Debt/equity for capital gearing

10. Increase in assets for growth

11. Increase in sales for growth

At the second stage, the publication uses six different criteria for judging the companies. These are: earning before depreciation, interest and tax/net assets, profit after tax/net worth; growth in assets, growth in sales, gross profit/sales, cash plough back/net worth.

Let us see what criteria (quantitative) companies use for measuring their performance. Exhibit presents criteria used by Hindustan Lever Limited.

Exhibit

Hindustan Lever: Use of quantitative criteria for performance measurement

In terms of ratios:

1. Profit after tax/sales

2. Earning per share (EPS)

3. Dividend per share (DPS)

4. Gross gearing-debt/equity

5. Interest cover (times)

6. Return on capital employed (RGCE)

7. Return on net worth (RONW)

8. Fixed assets turnover.(times)

9. Working capital turnover (times)

In Absolute Terms

1. Sales

2. Exports

3. Contribution to exchequer

4. Market price of share

5. Market capitalization

The company uses these criteria for ten years on comparative Besides, the company uses various qualitative criteria also. Exhibit presents the criteria used by Reliance Industries to measure its performance.

Exhibit

Reliance Industries: Criteria used for performance measurement

In terms of ratios:

1. Sales per share
2. Net profit margin
3. Earning per share
4. Cash earning per share
5. Book value per share
6. Debt: equity ratio
7. EBDIT/sales
8. Return on net worth
9. Equity dividend
10. Payout ratio

In absolute terms

1. Total sales
2. Export and deemed export
3. Taxes paid to the Government
4. Market capitalization

Management by Exception One of the most important ways of tailoring controls for efficiency effectiveness is to make sure that they are designed to point out exception In other words, by concentrating on exceptions from planned performance controls based on the time-honoured exception principle allow managers detect those places where their attention is required and should be give. This implies the use of management by exception particularly in controlling aspect. Management by exception is a system of identification a communication that signals to the manager when his attention is needed. From this point of view, management by exception can be used in other management processes also though its primary focus revolves around controlling.

Management by exception has six basic ingredients: measurement, projection, selection, observation, comparison, and decision-making.

1. Measurement assigns values to past and present performances: This is necessary because without measurement of some kind, it would be impossible to identify an exception.

2. Projection analyses those measurements that are meaningful to organisational objectives and extends them into future expectations.

3. Selection involves the criteria which management will use to follow progress towards organisational objectives.

4. Observation stage of management by exception involves measurement of current performance so that managers are aware of the current state of affairs in the organisation.

5. Comparison stage makes comparison of actual and planned performance and identifies the exceptions that require attention and reports the variances to management.

6. Decision-making prescribes the action that must be taken in order to bring performance back into control or to adjust expectations to reflect changing conditions, or to exploit opportunity.

Thus, it can be observed that management by exception is inseparable from other management essentials in many ways. However, the major difference lies in the fact that the superior's attention is drawn only in the case of exceptional differences between planned performance and actual performance. In other cases, decisions are taken by subordinate manager. However, what is exceptional requires the completion of whole process.

Benefits of Management by Exception

There are various areas where precepts of management by exception are used such as statistical control of product quality, economic order quantities and order points for control of inventories and supplies, break-even points for determining operating levels, trends in ratios of indirect to direct labour used in apportioning overhead, attitude surveys for gauging employee morale, etc. The use of management by exception is prevalent because of the following factors:

1. Management by exception saves executives' time because they apply themselves on fewer problems which are important. Other details of the problems are left to subordinates.

2. It concentrates executives' efforts on major problems. Instead of spreading managerial attention across all sorts of problems, it is placed selectively where and when it is needed. Thus, it ensures better utilization of managerial talents.

3. It facilitates better delegation of authority, increases. Span of management and consequently provides better opportunities for self-motivated personnel in the

organisation. It lessens the frequency of decisions at the higher levels of management which can concentrate on.

Strategic Control

Strategic control is a term used to describe the process used by organizations to control the formation and execution of strategic plans; it is a specialized form of management control, and differs from other forms of management control (in particular from operational control) in respects of its need to handle uncertainty and ambiguity at various points in the control process.

Definition

Julian and Scifres defines strategic control as follows

"Strategic control involves the monitoring and evaluation of plans, activities, and results with a view towards future action, providing a warning signal through diagnosis of data, and triggering appropriate interventions, be they either tactical adjustment or strategic reorientation."

Concept of Strategic Control

There are two aspects in this phase of strategic management: evaluation which emphasizes measurement of results of a strategic action and control which emphasizes on taking necessary actions in the light of gap that exists between intended results and actual results in the strategic action. However, because of on-going nature of strategic evaluation and control process.Both these are intertwined. In practice. The term control is used in a broad sense which includes evaluative aspect too because unless the results of an action are known, control actions cannot be taken.

Before we proceed further.it is worthwhile to make a comparison of strategic and operational control because the emphasis in both differs though an integrated control system may contain both.

Strategic and Operational Control

Strategic control is the process of taking into account the changing assumptions. both external and internal to the organisation on which a strategy is based, continually evaluating the strategy as it is being implemented and taking corrective actions to adjust strategy according to changing conditions or taking necessary actions to realign strategy implementation. For strategic evaluation and control following questions are relevant:

1. Are the premises made during the strategy formulation process proving to be correct?

2. Is the strategy being implemented properly?

3. Is there any need for change in the strategy? If yes, what is the type of change required to ensure strategic effectiveness?

Operational control focuses on the results of strategic action and is aimed at evaluating the performance of the organisation as a while, different SBUs and other units. The relevant questions for operational control are:

1. How is the organisation performing?

2. Are the organisational resources being utilised properly?

3. What are the actions required to ensure the proper utilization of resources in order to meet organisational objectives?

Strategic control and operational control both differ from each other in terms of their aim. main concern. focus. time horizon, and techniques used.

Difference between Strategic and Operational Control

Attribute	Strategic control	Operational control
1. Basic question	Are we moving in right direction	How are we performing?
2 Aim	Proactive, continuous questioning of the basicdirection of strategy	Allocation and use of resources organisational resources
3.Main concern	Steering the future direction of the organisation	Action control
4. Focus	External environment	Internal organisation
5. Time horizon	Long-term	Short-term
6. Exercise of control	Exclusively by top management, may be through lower-level support	Mainly by executive or middle management or the direction of top management
7. Main techniques,	Environmental scanning information gathering, questioning and review	Budgets, schedules and MBO

Barriers in Strategic Evaluation and Control

Strategic evaluation and control being an appraisal process for the organisation as a whole and people who are involved in strategic management process either at the stage of strategy formulation or strategy implementation or both, is not free from certain barriers and problems. These barriers and problems centre around two factors: motivational and operational. Let us see what these problems are and how these problems may be overcome.

Motivational Problems

The first problem in strategic evaluation is the motivation of managers (strategists) to evaluate whether they have chosen correct strategy after its results are available. Often two problem; are involved in motivation to evaluate the strategy: psychological problem and lack of direct relationship between performance and rewards.

1. Psychological Barriers

Managers are seldom motivated to evaluate their strategies because of the psychological barriers of accepting their mistakes. The strategy is formulated by top management which is very conscious about its sense of achievement. It hardly appreciates any mistake it may community at the level of strategy formulation. Even if something goes wrong at the level of strategy formulation, it may put the blame on the operating management and tries to find out the faults at the level of strategy implementation. This over-conscious approach of top management may prevent the objective review of whether correct strategy has been chosen and implemented. This may result into delay in taking correct alterative action and bringing the organisation back at satisfactory level. This happens more in the case of retrenchment strategy, particularly divestment strategy where a particular business has failed because of strategic mistake and in order to save the organisation from further damage, the business has to be sold.

2. Lack of Direct Relationship between Performance and Rewards

Another problem in motivation to review strategy is' the lack of direct relationship between performance achievement and incentives. It is true that performance achievement itself is a source of motivation but this cannot always happen. Such a situation hardly motivates the managers to review their strategy correctly. This happens more in the case of family-managed businesses Where professional managers are treated as outsiders and top positions, particularly at the board level, are reserved for insiders. Naturally very bright managers are not' motivated to review correctness or otherwise of their strategy. The family managers of such organisations are even more prone to psychological problem of not reviewing their strategy and admit their mistakes. Thus, what is required for motivating managers to evaluate their performance and strategy is the right type of motivational climate in the organisation. This climate can be set by linking performance and rewards as closely as possible. This linking is required not only for the top level but for the lower down in the organisation too. Many forward-looking companies.though few in .number, have taken this step when they have adopted the policy of taking board members from outside their families and friend groups. These companies have taken this- step not only to satisfy the requirements of financial institutions of broad basing the directorship but they have taken this step to motivate their top level managers. Naturally top managers in such companies can take any step to fulfill the organisational requirements including the evaluation of their strategy.

Operational Problems

Even if managers agree to evaluate the strategy, the problem of strategic evaluation is not over, though a beginning has been made. This is so because strategic evaluation is a nebulous process; many factors are not as clear as the managers would like these to be. These factors are in the areas of determination of evaluative criteria, performance measurement, and taking suitable corrective actions. All these are involved in strategic evaluation and control. However, nebulousness nature is not unique to strategic evaluation and control only but it is unique to the entire strategic management process. We shall make an attempt later in this chapter as to how these operational problems may be overcome

Role of Strategic Evaluation and Control

Strategic evaluation and control, though very important phase of strategic management, is often overlooked by strategists on the premise that once they have formulated a strategy and implemented, their role in strategic management is over. They remain mired with daily control reports which can be taken even at lower levels. This approach may be alright when there is not high stake involved in a strategy but fatal when the stake is high. Without strategic evaluation and control, strategists have no means to measure whether the chosen strategy is working properly or not. When strategic evaluation and control is undertaken properly, it contributes in three specific areas:

1. Measurement of organisational progress
2. Feedback for future actions, and
3. Linking performance and rewards

Measurement of Organisational Progress

Evaluation and control measures organisational progress towards achievement of its objectives. When a strategy is chosen, it specifies the likely outcomes which are relevant for achieving organisational objectives. The strategy is not an end in itself; it is a means for achieving something valuable to organisational success. Therefore, measuring this success as a result of strategy implementation is a prime concern for every strategist. This measurement should be undertaken during the process of strategy implementation as well as after implementation to ensure the progress as quickly as possible so that remedial actions are taken at appropriate time.

Feedback for Future Action

Strategic management being a continuous process with no apparent beginning and end, evaluation and control provides clues for recycling various actions which are relevant for achieving organisational objectives. This is possible only when strategic planning and control are well integrated. How control as a feedback mechanism helps in future course of action

Thus, control activities are undertaken in the light of criteria set by a strategic plan. But at the same time, control provides inputs either for adjusting the same strategic plan or taking future strategic plans. This is the way organisations progress over the period of time. They take a strategic action, implement it, and find its results. If the results are in tune with what intended the similar types of strategic actions are taken in future. Thus, there is a chain of strategic plan actions and control.

Linking Performance and Reward

This is the most crucial aspect of strategic evaluation and control but many organisations fail in linking performance and reward. This happens not only at the level of different organisations but even for a country as a whole. For exampleAbegglen has observed that "the dispension of part of the rewards by the organisations without regard to performances is more common in the less modem parts of the country than in the more advance ones, and in less developed than in more developed countries. It is one of the reasons why organisational control is less effective in less developed countries. Thus; linking performance and reward is a big issue. If taken objectively, evaluation and control provides inputs for relating performance and reward. This linking is vital for motivating organisational personnel more so in an era when there is not only fight for market share but for human talent too. A performance-based motivation system works better than the one which considers factors other than performance.

Control Process

Control, particularly operational control is exercised by a process consisting of four major steps as shown in Figure

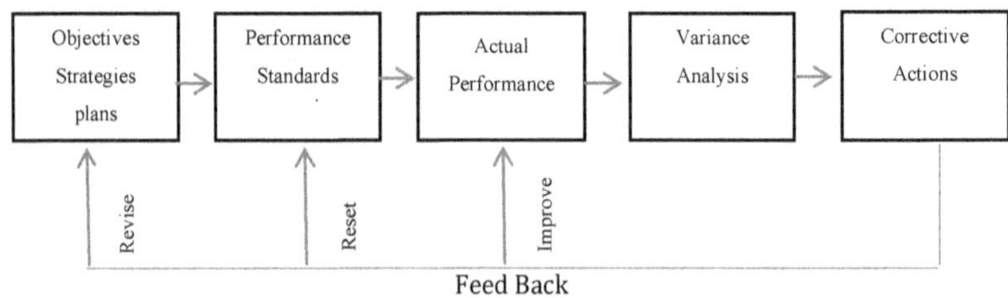

In order to exercise control, managers have to take four steps as indicated in Figure. These steps are as follows:

1. Setting performance standards
2. Measuring actual performance
3. Analyzing variance
4. Taking corrective actions.

Setting Performance Standards

Every function in the organisations begins with plans which are goals, objectives, or targets to be achieved. In the light of these, standards are established which are criteria against which actual results are measured.For setting standards for control purposes, it is important to identify clearly and precisely the results which are desired. Precision in the statement of these standards is important. In many areas, great precision is possible. However, in some areas, standards are less precise. Standards may be precise if they are set in quantities-physical, such as volume of products, man hour or monetary, such as costs, revenues, investment. They may also be in qualitative terms which measure performance.

After setting the standards, it is also important to decide about the level of achievement or performance which will be regarded as good or satisfactory. There are several characteristics of a particular work that determine good performance. Important characteristics which should be considered while determining any level of performance as good for some operations are: (i) output, (ii) expense, and (iii) resources. Expense refers to services or functions which may be expressed in quantity, for achieving a particular level of output. Resources refer to capital expenditure, human resources, etc. *after* identifying these characteristics, the desired level of each characteristic is determined. The desired level of performance should be reasonable and feasible. The level should have some amount of flexibility also, and should be stated in terms of range-maximum and minimum.

Measuring Actual Performance

The second major step ill. Control process is the measurement of performance. The step involves measuring the performance in respect of a work in terms of control standards. The presence of standard implies a corresponding ability to observe and comprehend the nature of existing conditions and to ascertain the degree of control being achieved.

The measurement of performance against standards should be on a future basis, so that deviations may be detected in advance of their actual occurrence and avoided by appropriate actions. Appraisal of actual or expected performance becomes an easy task, if standards are properly determined and methods of measuring performance which can be expressed in physical and monetary terms, such as production units, sales volume, profits, etc. can be easily and precisely measurable. The performance which is qualitative and intangible, such as human relations, employee morale, etc. cannot be measured precisely. For such purposes, techniques like psychological tests and opinion surveys may be applied. Such techniques draw heavily from intuitive judgment and experience, and these tools are fat" from exact. According to Peter Drucker, it is very much desirable to have clear and common measurements in all key areas of business. It is not necessary that measurements are rigidly quantitative. In his opinion, for measuring tangible and intangible performance, measurement must be (i) clear, simple, and rational, (ii) relevant, (iii) direct attention and efforts, and (iv) reliable, self-announcing, and understandable without complicated interpretation or philosophical discussions.

Analysing Variance

The third major step in control process is the comparison of actual and standard performance. It involves two steps: (i) finding out the extent of deviations, and (ii) identifying the causes of such deviations. When adequate standards are developed and actual performance is measured accurately, any variation will be clearly revealed. Management may have information relating to work performance, data, charts, graphs and written reports, besides personal observation to keep itself informed about performance in different segments of the organisation. Such performance is compared with the standard to find out whether the various segments and individuals of the organisation are progressing in the right direction.

When the standards are achieved, no further managerial action is necessary and control process is complete. However, standards may not be achieved in all cases and the extent of variations may differ from case to case. Naturally, management is required to determine whether strict compliance with standards is required or there should be a permissible limit of variation (Figure) In fact, there cannot be any uniform practice for determining such variations. Such variations depend upon the type of activity. For example, a very minute variation in engineering products may be significant than a wide variation in other activities.

When the deviation between standard and actual performance is beyond the prescribed limit, an analysis is made of the causes of such deviations. For controlling and planning purposes, ascertaining the causes of variations along with computation of variations is important because such analysis helps management in taking up proper control action. The analysis will pinpoint the causes which ate controllable by the person re-possible. In such a case, person concerned will take necessary corrective action.

However.if the variation is caused by uncontrollable factors the person concerned cannot be held responsible and he cannot take any action.

Measurement of performance.' analysis of deviations and their causes may be of no use unless these are communicated to the person who can take corrective action. Such communication is presented generally in the form of a report showing performance standard. actual performance, deviations between those two, tolerance limits, and causes for deviations. As soon as possible. Reports containing control information should be sent to the person whose performance is being measured and controlled. The underlying philosophy is that the person who is responsible for a job can have a better influence on final results by his own action. A summary of the control report should be given to the superior concerned because the person on the job may either need help of his superior in improving the performance or may need warning for his failure. In addition, other people who may be interested in control reports are (i) executives engaged in formulating new plans: and (ii) staff personnel who are expected to be familiar with control information for giving any advice about the activity under control when approached.

Taking Corrective Actions

This is the last step in the control process which requires that actions should be taken to maintain the desired degree of control in the system or operation. An organisation is not a self-regulating system such as thermostat which operates in a state of equilibrium put there by engineering design. In a business organisation, this type of automatic control cannot be established because the state of affairs that exists is the result of so many factors in the total environment. Thus some additional actions are required to maintain the control. Such actions may be on the following lines:

1. Improvement in the performance by taking suitable actions if the performance is not up to the mark: or
2. Resetting the performance standards if these are too high and unrealistic; or
3. Change the objectives, strategies and plans if these are not workable.

5.4. Quantitative and Qualitative Factors

While quantitative factors have been and will continue to be very important in the site selection process, qualitative factors are also critical in order to ensure that the company makes the best decision. This is particularly true as the economies of the United States and the world become more knowledge-based. The list will vary depending on type of facility (i.e. manufacturing, logistics, research & technology, office), but most factors apply to all forms of projects. Please find below a summary of the most important quantitative and qualitative factors considered by companies.

Quantitative Factors

1. Property Tax Rates
2. Corporate Income Tax Rates
3. Sales Tax Rates
4. Real Estate Costs
5. Utility Rates
6. Average Wage/Salary Levels
7. Construction Costs
8. Worker's Compensation Rates
9. Unemployment Compensation Rates
10. Personal Income Tax Rates
11. Industry Sector Labor Pool Size
12. Infrastructure Development Costs
13. Education Achievement Levels
14. Crime Statistics
15. Frequency of Natural Disasters
16. Cost of Living Index
17. Number of Commercial Flights to Key Markets
18. Proximity to Major Key Geographic Markets
19. Unionization Rate/Right to Work versus Non-Right to Work State
20. Population of Geographic Area

Qualitative Factors

1. Level of Collaboration with Government, Educational and Utility Officials
2. Sports, Recreational and Cultural Amenities
3. Confidence in Ability of All Parties to Meet Company's Deadlines
4. Political Stability of Location
5. Climate
6. Availability of Quality Healthcare
7. Chemistry of Project Team with Local and State Officials
8. Perception of Quality of Professional Services Firms to Meet the Company's Need
9. Predictability of Long-term Operational Costs
10. Ability to Complete Real Estate Due Diligence Process Quickly

Important part of the site selection evaluation process relates to the weighting of the key quantitative and qualitative factors. Depending on the type of project, factors will be weighted differently. As an example, for a new manufacturing facility project, issues such as utility rates, real estate costs, property tax rates, collaboration with governmental entities, and average hourly wage rates may be weighted more heavily. By contract, for a new office facility factors such as real estate costs, number of commercial flights, crime statistics, climate and industry sector labor pool size may be more important.

When assisting clients, our firm weights the importance of each criterion. We then rate the risk level of each factor. Finally, we input the weighted data into a formula to compute a score for each site. This approach allows Ginovus to tailor the analysis to meet each client's needs and to adjust the formula as issues arise. We believe this allows us to provide the best possible recommendation to a client. Every project is unique and must be evaluated based upon its own individual set of circumstances. By identifying the key factors impacting a project, site selection advisors and companies can reach an informed decision. Carefully designed methodology, when combined with thorough analysis, and sometimes instinct, should lead to a successful outcome.

5.5.   Strategy Evaluation

Strategy Evaluation is as significant as strategy formulation because it throws light on the efficiency and effectiveness of the comprehensive plans in achieving the desired results. The managers can also assess the appropriateness of the current strategy in today's dynamic world with socio-economic, political and technological innovations. Strategic Evaluation is the final phase of strategic management.

The Process of Strategy Evaluation

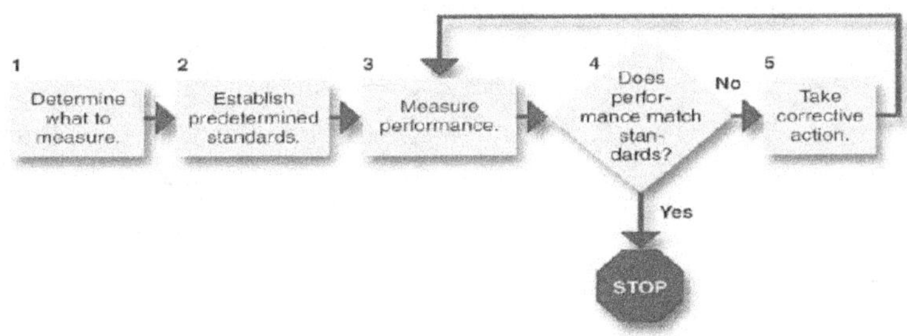

1. Determine what to Measure

This involves clarification of the aims to be achieved, i.e. the aims and objectives must be stated in clear terms that should include specific deadlines

2. Establish Standard of Performance

Requires realistic measurement by which the degree and quality of goal achievement can be determined.

3. Measure Actual Performance

This should be an ongoing repetitive process, actual frequency of measurement being dependent on the type of activity

4. Comparing Actual Performance against Standards

This involves comparing measured results with established targets or standards previously set.

5. Take Corrective Action

If actual results fall outside the desired tolerance rang, action must be taken to rectify the deviation

5.6.　Categories of Evaluation

According to the criterion of the purpose of evaluation, it is classified into the following categories:

- Strategic evaluation (with the purpose to assess and analyze the evolution of NSRF and OP with respect to national and Community priorities);
- Operational evaluation (with the purpose to support the process of NSRF and OP monitoring).

Strategic evaluation concerns mainly the analysis and assessment of interventions at the level of strategic goals. The object of strategic evaluation consists of the analysis and appraisal of the relevance of general directions of interventions determined at the programming stage. One of the significant aspects of strategic evaluation consists of the verification of the adopted strategy with respect to the current and anticipated social and economic situation.

Operational evaluation is closely linked to the process of NSRF and OP management and monitoring. The purpose of operational evaluation consists of providing support to the institutions responsible for the implementation of NSRF and OP with regards to the achievement of the assumed operational objectives by providing practically useful conclusions and recommendations. According to Regulation 1083/2006, operational evaluation should be carried out, in particular, in the case when monitoring has revealed significant deviations from the originally assumed objectives and when requests are submitted for the review of an operational programme or its part.

Criteria for Evaluation

A strategy should be continuously evaluated. The criteria that can be used for evaluating strategy are:

1. Consistency:A strategy should not have inconsistent objectives. Inconsistencies are reflected by:
2. Conflicts and interdepartmental bickering. Conflicts are people-based rather than issue based.
3. Sub optimization where one department tries to gain success over others.
4. Top management spending lot of time in solving problems and issues.

   - Consonance: If refers to set of treads or individual trends that need examination to evaluate strategy. The strategy should be adaptive capabilities in terms of abilities, competencies, skills and talents to carry out a strategy.
   - A strategy must provide strategic advantage. It result from superiority in resources, skills or position. Size can provide positional advantage. The nature of positional advantage in relation to competitors should be examined for evaluation a strategy.

CHAPTER VI

OTHER STRATEGIC ISSUES

6.1.   Managing Technology and Innovation

Technological change is a combination of two activities invention and innovation. Invention is the development of a new idea that has useful applications. Innovation is a more complex term, referring to how an invention is brought into commercial usage. The distinction between the two is very important. As an example, Henry Ford did not invent the automobile; companies in Europe such as Daimler were producing cars well before Ford founded his company. Henry Ford instead focused on the innovation of automobiles, creating a method (mass production) by which cars could be manufactured and distributed cheaply to a large number of customers.

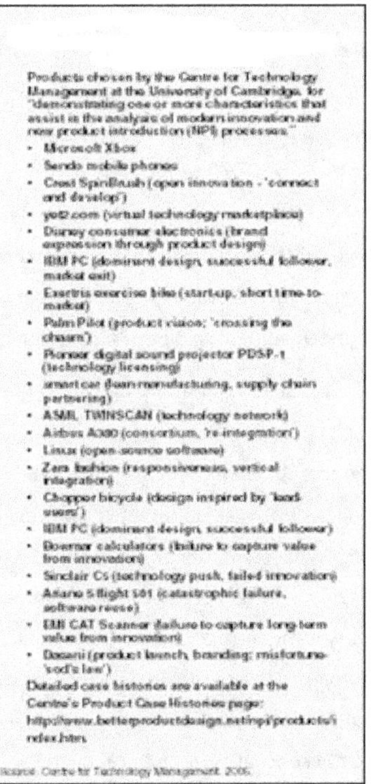

Figure 1: Examples of Technological Innovation and Market Growth

Source: Centre for Technology Management, 2005.

The practice of technology management and the development of technology strategy require an understanding of the different forms of innovation and the features of each form.

- Incremental innovations exploit the potential of established designs, and often reinforce the dominance of established firms. They improve the existing functional capabilities of a technology by means of small-scale improvements in the technology's value, adding attributes such as performance, safety, quality, and cost.

- Generational or next-generation technology innovations are incremental innovations that lead to the creation of a new but not radically different system.

- Radical innovations introduce new concepts that depart significantly from past practices and help create products or processes based on a different set of engineering or scientific principles and often open up entirely new markets and potential applications. They provide new functional capabilities unavailable in previous versions of the product or service.

- Architectural innovations serve to extend the radical-incremental classification of innovation and introduce the notion of changes in the way in which the components of a product or system are linked together.

There are two important steps required to properly manage corporate innovation. First is to correctly identify a project as a new product vs. a technological innovation, so a proper development process can be used (the first may be a more traditional stage-gate process; the second should be more cyclical and iterative). Second, managers need to identify what category an innovation falls under, since each type of innovation has its own challenges.

For example, In the aircraft industry, an improvement in the construction of a wing is an incremental innovation. Such a new technology can be introduced relatively easily and integrated with existing products. An example of a generational innovation is the introduction of the Boeing 777, a new class of aircraft different from previous models. While similar in appearance to the 767 and its predecessor, the 777 introduced a whole new set of technologies and capabilities, requiring tremendous investment by Boeing and its business partners. A radical innovation in aircraft was the introduction of the jet engine, which completely changed the performance of aircraft compared to propeller-driven airplanes. Finally, the concept of a flying machine as envisioned by the Wright Brothers exemplifies an architectural innovation. Prior to the Wright brothers, the concept of mechanical flight had been invented and discussed. The Wright brothers actually developed and demonstrated a design that made human flight a reality.

Innovation Management

Invention is an activity often identified with a single engineer or scientist working alone in a laboratory until he or she happens upon an idea that will change the world, like the light bulb. In reality, industrial invention, at least since the time of Edison, has involved many people working together in a collaborative setting to create new technology. Innovation requires an even broader set of people, including manufacturing engineers, marketing and sales managers, investors and financial managers, and business strategists. The methods for organizing this set of people to bring a new idea from the laboratory to the marketplace form the basis of the discipline of innovation management. Innovation traditionally has been viewed as a linear process, which involves several stages in sequence: research, development, manufacturing, marketing, and ultimately, reaching the customer.

In each step, a group of employees take the idea as it is passed to them from the previous stage, modify it to accomplish a specific function, and pass it on to the next stage. Each team involved in the process has a clear function. Researchers are responsible for creating a working demonstration of the technology, developers and engineers turn it into something that can be produced, manufacturing engineers actually turn out the product, and marketers sell it to customers.

This linear model of innovation has proven to be a misconception of the process, however. For example, problems during the manufacturing process may require researchers to go back and change the technology to facilitate production.

The technology may reach the marketing stage, only to turn out to be something no one wants to buy. Technology cannot be handed off between stages like a baton in a relay race. In any case, managing innovation in a sequential process would take a very long time, especially if each stage needs to perfect the technology before it can move on to the next stage.

6.2.   Mergers and Acquisitions

Mergers and Acquisitions are part of strategic management of any business. It involves consolidation of two businesses with an aim to increase market share, profits and influence in the industry. Mergers and Acquisitions are complex processes which require preparing, analysis and deliberation. There are a lot of parties who might be affected by a merger or an acquisition, like government agencies, workers and managers. Before a deal is finalized all party needs to be taken into consideration, and their concerns should be addressed, so that any possible hurdles can be avoided.

Introduction to Mergers &Acquisitions

'Mergers and Acquisitions' is a technical term used to define the consolidation of companies. When two companies are combined to form a single unit, it is known as merger, while an acquisition refers to the purchase of company by another one, which means that no new company is formed, but one company has been absorbed into another. Mergers and Acquisitions are important component of strategic management, which comes under corporate finance. The subject deals with buying, selling, dividing and combining various companies. It is a type of restructuring, with the aim to grow rapidly, increase profitability and capture a greater proportion of a market share.

Parties in an Acquisition

The Target Company is the company that is being acquired.

The Acquirer company is the company that is acquiring the target.

Mergers can be Dividedinto Three Types

Horizontal merger: It happens when both companies are in the same line of business, which means they are usually competitors. Example: Disney bought LucasFilm. Both companies were involved in production of film, TV shows.

Vertical merger: This happens when two companies are in the same line of production, but stage of production is different. Example: Microsoft bought Nokia to support its software and provide hardware necessary for the smartphone.

Conglomerate merger: This happens when the two companies are in totally different line of business. Example, Berkshire Hathaway acquired Lubrizol. This kind of merger mostly takes place in order to diversify and spread the risks, in case the current business stops yielding adequate profits.

Introduction to M&A

The main difference between a merger and an acquisition is that a merger is a form of legal consolidation of two companies, which are formed into a single entity, while an acquisition happens when one company is absorbed by another company, which means that the company that is purchasing the other company continues to exist. In the recent years, the distinction between the two has become more and more blurred, as companies have started doing joint ventures. Sometimes acquirer wants to keep the name of the acquired company, as it has goodwill value attached to it.

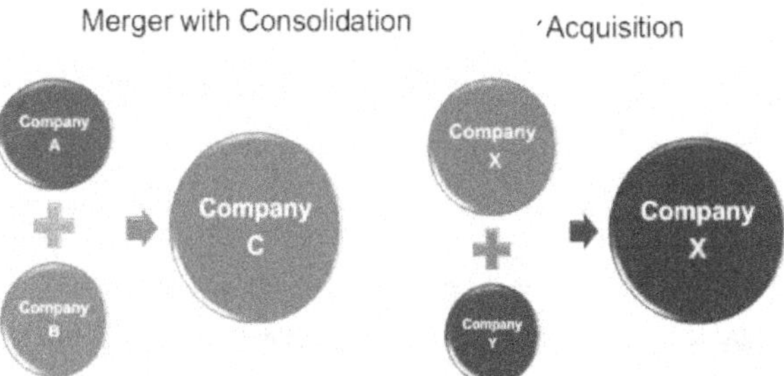

Mergers and acquisitions are complex area of a company long-term strategy. The process takes a long time, at times, even years. It involves number of parties and stakeholders:

The two companies which are being merged or coordinating to venture are the main stakeholders, since any changes in the structure of the company is likely impact both companies.

Employees will also be affected, since they are an integral part of the companies. At times, during a merger or acquisition employees have to be laid off.

The government agencies play a decisive role in any merger or acquisition, as they want to make sure that the M&A does not create a monopoly or impinge on the rights of general public. Any merger of acquisition must not be a hurdle to competitive environment in the industry.

Pressure Groups would be interested in the impact the merger or acquisition would have on the environment, worker welfare, consumer welfare and overall social impact the collusion. Some companies manufacture product/services that are controversial, hence detested by some people. Firms must find a way to deal with possible hostility from these people.

Competitors would be interested in a possible merger or acquisition between two companies in the industry, since a collusion could threaten to take away their market share as the combined company would be more powerful, financially and strategically.

Financial institutions also have a stake in possible merger or acquisition, since the companies involved might have outstanding debt. Alternatively, a company involved in a post-merger or an acquisition might want to borrow more money, so that the financial institutions would have to evaluate the company's financial standing and ability to repay it later.Three important considerations should be taken into account:

- The company must be willing to take the risk and vigilantly make investments to benefit fully from the merger as the competitors and the industry take heed quickly

- To reduce and diversify risk, multiple bets must be made, in order to narrow down to the one that will prove fruitful
- The management of the acquiring firm must learn to be resilient, patient and be able to adopt to the change owing to ever-changing business dynamics in the industry

Stages Involved in any M&A

Phase 1: Pre-acquisition review: this would include self assessment of the acquiring company with regards to the need for M&A, ascertain the valuation (undervalued is the key) and chalk out the growth plan through the target.

Phase 2: Search and screen targets: This would include searching for the possible apt takeover candidates. This process is mainly to scan for a good strategic fit for the acquiring company.

Phase 3: Investigate and valuation of the target: Once the appropriate company is shortlisted through primary screening, detailed analysis of the target company has to be done. This is also referred to as due diligence.

Phase 4: Acquire the target through negotiations: Once the target company is selected, the next step is to start negotiations to come to consensus for a negotiated merger or a bear hug. This brings both the companies to agree mutually to the deal for the long term working of the M&A.

Phase 5:Post merger integration: If all the above steps fall in place, there is a formal announcement of the agreement of merger by both the participating companies.

Reasons for the Failure of M&A–Analyzed during the Stages of M&A

Poor strategic fit: Wide difference in objectives and strategies of the company

Poorly managed Integration: Integration is often poorly managed without planning and design. This leads to failure of implementation

Incomplete due diligence: Inadequate due diligence can lead to failure of M&A as it is the crux of the entire strategy

Overly optimistic: Too optimistic projections about the target company leads to bad decisions and failure of the M&A

Example: Breakdown in merger discussions between IBM and Sun Microsystems happened due to disagreement over price and other terms.

Recent M&A

Acquirer	Target Company	Deal Size	Comments
Flipkart	Myntra	USD300mn	Acquisition led to scripting of largest ecommerce stories
Asian Paints	Ess Ess bathroom products	undisclosed	to be one stop provider in home décor space
RIL	Network 18 Media & Investments	Rs4000cr	78% percent shares were taken over by RIL
Merck	Sigma	USD17bn	Acquisition to boost lab supply business of Merck
Sun Pharma	Ranbaxy	USD4bn	increase presence in global and domestic markets
TCS	CMC		merger to consolidate IT business
Tata Power	PT Arutmin Indonesia	Rs 47.4bn	Purchased 30% stake
Groupe Lactalis	Tirumala Milk	USD275mn	lactalis entry into India
CSP CX	Aditya Birla Minacs	USD260mn	Aditya Birla's exit from IT industry
Thomas Cook	Sterling India	Rs 870cr	Entry into hospitality business
Yahoo	Bookpad	USD15mn	First acquisition made by Yahoo
Kotak Bank	ING Vysya	USD2.4bn	All share deal
Ola cabs	Taxi for sure	USD200mn	Acquisition of competition

6.3. Diversification

Diversification strategies are used to extend the company's product lines and operate in several different markets. The general strategies include concentric, horizontal and conglomerate diversification.

Each strategy focuses on a specific method of diversification. The concentric strategy is used when a firm wants to increase its products portfolio to include like products produced within the same company, the horizontal strategy is used when the company wants to produce new products in a similar market, and the conglomerate diversification strategy is used when a company starts operating in two or more unrelated industries.

Diversification strategies help to increase flexibility and maintain profit during sluggish economic periods.

Warren Buffet on Diversification

"Diversification is protection against ignorance, it makes little sense for those who know what they're doing."

Concentric Diversification

A concentric diversification strategy lets a firm to add similar products to an already established business. For example, when a computer company producing personal computers using towers starts to produce laptops, it uses concentric strategies. The technical knowledge for new venture comes from its current field of skilled employees.

Concentric diversification strategies are rampant in the food production industry. For example, a ketchup manufacturer starts producing salsa, using its current production facilities.

Horizontal Diversification

Horizontal diversification allow a firm to start exploring other zones in terms of product manufacturing. Companies depend on current market share of loyal customers in this strategy. When a television manufacturer starts producing refrigerators, freezers and washers or dryers, it uses horizontal diversification.

A downside is the company's dependence on one group of consumers. The company has to leverage on the brand loyalty associated with current products. This is dangerous since new products may not garner the same favor as the company's other products.

Conglomerate Diversification

In conglomerate diversification strategies, companies will look to enter a previously untapped market. This is often done using mergers and acquisitions.

Moving into a new industry is highly dangerous, due to unfamiliarity with the new industry. Brand loyalty may also be reduced when quality is not managed. However, this strategy offers increasing flexibility in reaching new economic markets.

For example, a company into automotive repair parts may enter the toy production industry. Each company allows for a broader base of customers. There is an opportunity of income when one industry's sales falter.

Companies often need to downsize themselves to be lean and compete better against stiff competition. The idea is to make a more productive company incur lesser costs. There are mainly two major ways to downsize, known as Retrenchment and Restructuring.

Retrenchment

In the early 20th century, battles in World War I, occurred in series of parallel trenches. If an attacking army forced the enemy to abandon a trench, the defenders used to move back to the next trench. The handy adjustments were far more preferable to losing the battle completely. Retrenchment, a popular business strategy now, owes its origin to this trench warfare. Firms that follow retrenchment strategy generally shrink one or more business units.

Retrenchment is accompanied often by laying off employees. This reduces the overall cost of management and provides a better way to manage the employees more productively. This type of strategy is best applicable to a saturated and low margin market such as groceries where retailers look to add non-food merchandise to their stocks to improve the bottom line.

Restructuring

Some better and more effective strategies are needed for some firms to survive and become successful in the future. **Divestment** means selling off a portion of the firm's operations. Sometimes, divestment usually reverses a forward vertical integration strategy, such as in the case where Ford sold Hertz. Divestment can also lead to reverse backward vertical integration.

General Motors (GM), once turned their parts supplier, called Delphi Automotive Systems Corporation, from the original GM subsidiary into a newly formed and independent firm. This was done via a spin-off, which includes creating a completely new company the stock of which is owned by investors. This often accompanies stock splits for large companies.

Divestment can also help the company to undo diversification strategies. Firms that have engaged in unrelated diversification find the diversification strategies more useful. Investors, however, often find it complex to understand the process of diversified firms, and this can result in relatively poor performance by the stocks of such firms. This is called **diversification discount.**

Executives sometimes break up diversified companies to derive the stock value. Sometimes, the operations of a firm have no value at all. When sale of a part of business is not possible, the best option may be **liquidation.** In liquidation, the parts that generate no value are simply shut down, often at a tremendous financial loss.

GM has liquidated its Geo, Saturn, Oldsmobile, and Pontiac brands. Such moves are painful as large portions of investments have to be written off, but becoming "leaner and meaner" may at least save the company from becoming obsolete.

6.4.   Global Issues and Challenges in Strategic Management

Business Process Reengineering

Business Process Reengineering involves the radical redesign of core business processes to achieve dramatic improvements in productivity, cycle times and quality. In Business Process Reengineering, companies start with a blank sheet of paper and rethink existing processes to deliver more value to the customer. They typically adopt a new value system that places increased emphasis on customer needs. Companies reduce organizational layers and eliminate unproductive activities in two key areas. First, they redesign functional organizations into cross-functional teams. Second, they use technology to improve data dissemination and decision making.

Steps in Business Process Reengineering

Business Process Reengineering is a dramatic change initiative that contains five major steps that managers should take:

- Refocus company values on customer needs
- Redesign core processes, often using information technology to enable improvements
- Reorganize a business into cross-functional teams with end-to-end responsibility for a process
- Rethink basic organizational and people issues
- Improve business processes across the organization

Uses of Business Process Reengineering

Companies use Business Process Reengineering to

- **Reduce costs and cycle times.** Business Process Reengineering reduces costs and cycle times by eliminating unproductive activities and the employees who perform them. Reorganization by teams decreases the need for management layers, accelerates information flows and eliminates the errors and rework caused by multiple handoffs.
- **Improve quality.** Business Process Reengineering improves quality by reducing the fragmentation of work and establishing clear ownership of processes. Workers gain responsibility for their output and can measure their performance based on prompt feedback

6.5. Total Quality Management

TQM is a management philosophy that seeks to integrate all organizational functions (marketing, finance, design, engineering, and production, customer service, etc.) to focus on meeting customer needs and organizational objectives.

TQM views an organization as a collection of processes. It maintains that organizations must strive to continuously improve these processes by incorporating the knowledge and experiences of workers. The simple objective of TQM is "Do the right things, right the first time, every time." TQM is infinitely variable and adaptable. Although originally applied to manufacturing operations, and for a number of years only used in that area, TQM is now becoming recognized as a generic management tool, just as applicable in service and public sector organizations. There are a number of evolutionary strands, with different sectors creating their own versions from the common ancestor.

TQM is the foundation for activities, which include:

- Commitment by senior management and all employees
- Meeting customer requirements
- Reducing development cycle times
- Just in time/demand flow manufacturing
- Improvement teams
- Reducing product and service costs
- Systems to facilitate improvement
- Line management ownership
- Employee involvement and empowerment
- Recognition and celebration
- Challenging quantified goals and benchmarking
- Focus on processes/improvement plans
- Specific incorporation in strategic planning

This shows that TQM must be practiced in all activities, by all personnel, in manufacturing, marketing, engineering, R&D, sales, purchasing, HR, etc.

Principles of TQM

Total quality management can be summarized as a management system for a customer-focused organization that involves all employees in continual improvement. It uses strategy, data, and effective communications to integrate the quality discipline into the culture and activities of the organization. Many of these concepts are present in modern Quality Management Systems, the successor to TQM. Here are the 8 principles of total quality management:

1. Customer-focused

The customer ultimately determines the level of quality. No matter what an organization does to foster quality improvement-training employees, integrating quality into the design process, upgrading computers or software, or buying new measuring tools—the customer determines whether the efforts were worthwhile.

2. Total Employee Involvement

All employees participate in working toward common goals. Total employee commitment can only be obtained after fear has been driven from the workplace, when empowerment has occurred, and management has provided the proper environment. High-performance work systems integrate continuous improvement efforts with normal business operations. Self-managed work teams are one form of empowerment.

3. Process-centered

A fundamental part of TQM is a focus on process thinking. A process is a series of steps that take inputs from suppliers (internal or external) and transforms them into outputs that are delivered to customers (again, either internal or external). The steps required to carry out the process are defined, and performance measures are continuously monitored in order to detect unexpected variation.

4. Integrated System

Although an organization may consist of many different functional specialties often organized into vertically structured departments, it is the horizontal processes interconnecting these functions that are the focus of TQM.

Micro-processes add up to larger processes, and all processes aggregate into the business processes required for defining and implementing strategy. Everyone must understand the vision, mission, and guiding principles as well as the quality policies, objectives, and critical processes of the organization. Business performance must be monitored and communicated continuously.

An integrated business system may be modeled after the Baldrige National Quality Program criteria and/or incorporate the ISO 9000 standards. Every organization has a unique work culture, and it is virtually impossible to achieve excellence in its products and services unless a good quality culture has been fostered. Thus, an integrated system connects business improvement elements in an attempt to continually improve and exceed the expectations of customers, employees, and other stakeholders.

5. Strategic and Systematic Approach

A critical part of the management of quality is the strategic and systematic approach to achieving an organization's vision, mission, and goals. This process, called strategic planning or strategic management, includes the formulation of a strategic plan that integrates quality as a core component.

6. Continual Improvement

A major thrust of TQM is continual process improvement. Continual improvement drives an organization to be both analytical and creative in finding ways to become more competitive and more effective at meeting stakeholder expectations.

7. Fact-based Decision Making

In order to know how well an organization is performing, data on performance measures are necessary. TQM requires that an organization continually collect and analyze data in order to improve decision making accuracy, achieve consensus, and allow prediction based on past history.

8. Communications

During times of organizational change, as well as part of day-to-day operation, effective communications plays a large part in maintaining morale and in motivating employees at all levels. Communications involve strategies, method, and timeliness.

These elements are considered so essential to TQM that many organizations define them, in some format, as a set of core values and principles on which the organization is to operate. The methods for implementing this approach come from the teachings of such quality leaders as Philip B. Crosby, W. Edwards Deming, Armand V. Feigenbaum, Kaoru Ishikawa, and Joseph M. Juran.

6.6. Benchmarking

Benchmarking is a way of discovering what is the best performance being achieved – whether in a particular company, by a competitor or by an entirely different industry. This information can then be used to identify gaps in an organization's processes in order to achieve a competitive advantage. Thus it is important for Six Sigma practitioners to:

- Understand fully the purpose and use of benchmarking.
- Understand the difference between benchmarking and competitor research.
- Gain insight to ensure that benchmarking is in alignment with the company's management objectives.

Benchmarking as a Tool

Benchmarking is a process for obtaining a measure – a benchmark. Simply stated, benchmarks are the "what," and benchmarking is the "how." But benchmarking is not a quick or simple process tool. Before undertaking a benchmarking opportunity, it is important to have a thorough understanding of the company's guidelines. Some companies have strict guidelines as to what information can be gathered, and whom practitioners can contact to get that information. Depending on the size of the company, practitioners may be surprised at what is readily available in-house.

Benchmarking is not just a matter of making inquiries to other companies or touring and documenting another company's facilities or processes. When making use of benchmarking, a company should not limit the scope to its own industry, nor should benchmarking be a one-time event.

Benchmarking Versus Competitor Research

While competitor research is neither a better nor a worse practice than benchmarking, the important thing is to understand that there is a difference between the two. Available time and resources will help decide which tool will add the most value. The following table represents experience in dealing with the two practices:

Differences Between Benchmarking and Competitor Research	
Benchmarking	**Competitor Research**
Focuses on best practices	Focuses on performance measures
Strives for continuous improvement	Bandage or quick fix
Partnering to share information	Considered corporate spying by some
Needed to maintain a competitive edge	Simply a "nice to have"
Adapting based on customer needs after examination of the best	Attempting to mirror another company/process

Three Primary Classifications of Benchmarking

Although there are many forms of benchmarking, they can be classified into three categories – internal, competitive and strategic.

Internal benchmarking is used when a company already has established and proven best practices and they simply need to share them. Again, depending on the size of the company, it may be large enough to represent a broad range of performance (i.e., cycle time for opening new accounts in branches coast to coast). Internal benchmarking also may be necessary if comparable industries are not readily available.

Competitive benchmarking is used when a company wants to evaluate its position within its industry. In addition, competitive benchmarking is used when a company needs to identify industry leadership performance targets.

Strategic benchmarking is used when identifying and analyzing world-class performance. This form of benchmarking is used most when a company needs to go outside of its own industry. Six Sigma often uses Hoshin to ensure that all employees are knowledgeable about the strategic direction for the company. Within a company's Hoshin plan, goals are established relative to benchmarks set by world-class organizations. Often, these benchmarks are obtained from outside industries.

Steps Involved in Benchmarking

It is important that Six Sigma practitioners have a thorough understanding of their own company's guidelines before undertaking a benchmarking opportunity. The following is a list of the vital few steps involved in benchmarking. These steps should be tailored based on company policies, resource availability and the project or process one is dealing with:

1. **Understand the company's current process performance gaps.** This will help decide what needs benchmarking.

2. **Obtain support and approval from the executive leadership team.** That approval and support will assist with eliminating roadblocks, providing adequate resources and expediting the benchmark-gathering process.

3. **Document benchmarking objectives and scope.** This is a necessity for any project.

4. **Document the current process.** Without up-to-date knowledge of the current process:

    *   Time and resources can be wasted collecting process documentation and data that already exists.

    *   The project may lack focus, purpose and/or depth.

    *   Benchmarking visits may appear to be random exercises in information-gathering.

    *   The team could select a partner whose performance is actually worse than that of its own organization.

    *   Collected benchmarking data will be difficult to compare "apples to apples" in terms of process requirements.

5. **Agree on the primary metrics.** Benchmarking measurements are used as the basis of many comparisons:

    *   To determine the gap between current performance and that of partner organizations.

    *   To track progress from the present (with the current process) into the future.

    *   To track partners' progress toward their goals.

    *   To determine superior performance with process improvements.

    *   To use a measurement systems analysis (MSA):

        i.   These comparisons will be valid only if everyone participating in the study measures performance in exactly the same way – every time.

        ii. It is important to make sure metrics are being established that potential benchmarking partners are probably already tracking or that can be easily derived from existing measurements.

6. **The metrics should be put in writing.** In particular:

    i.   What is being measured

    ii.   How the units of measure will be classified.

    iii.   What should be included in the measurement.

    iv.   What should not be included.

    v.   How to make any necessary calculations.

    vi.   Examples of typical measurements.

7. **Agree on what to benchmark.** Everyone must be in agreement on what to benchmark prior to any benchmark gathering initiative in order to:

    a.   Understand gaps of low performers.

    b.   Understand impact to customers, associates and shareholders.

    c.   Prioritize and select one to three metrics to benchmark.

8. **Develop a data collection plan.**

9. **Identify research sources and initiate data gathering.**

10. **Design a screening survey to assist with partner selection.** Characteristics of the survey are important:

- Crisp focus on indicators of excellence
- Two pages maximum
- 30 minutes maximum to complete
- Objective, multiple-choice questions
- Communicates the plans, objectives and resource requirements for the study
- Reflects focus areas for subsequent in-depth questionnaires

11. **Determine how to contact and screen companies.**

12. **Design a detailed survey to gather information.**

13. **Decide if gathered information meets original objectives.**

14. **Conduct a site visit.**

15. **Apply the learnings to performance gaps.**

16. **Communicate to the executive leadership to ensure continued support.**

17. **Develop a recommended implementation plan with process owner.**

18. **Know when to update and recalibrate.**

External Resources for Benchmarking

Some may find it surprising that there is a world of benchmarking information already gathered and available. While there may be a fee associated with obtaining this information, the fee can easily be offset by the savings in time and resources that come from not having to gather the benchmarking information needed to meet agreed-upon objectives. Here are some available sources:

a. American Productivity & Quality Center (APQC)
b. APQC Knowledge Sharing Network
c. The Benchmarking Exchange
d. Best Practices, LLC & Global Benchmarking Council

6.7. Six Sigma

Sigma represents the population standard deviation, which is a measure of the variation in a data set collected about the process. If a defect is defined by specification limits separating good from bad outcomes of a process, then a six sigma process has a process mean (average) that is six standard deviations from the nearest specification limit. This provides enough buffer between the process natural variation and the specification limits.

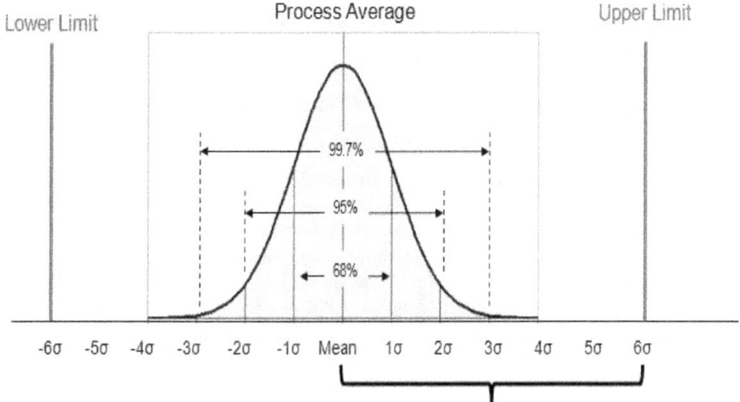

For example, if a product must have a thickness between 10.32 and 10.38 inches to meet customer requirements, then the process mean should be around 10.35, with a standard deviation less than 0.005 (10.38 would be 6 standard deviations away from 10.35).

Six Sigma can also be thought of as a measure of process performance, with Six Sigma being the goal, based on the defects per million. Once the current performance of the process is measured, the goal is to continually improve the sigma level striving towards 6 sigma. Even if the improvements do not reach 6 sigma, the improvements made from 3 sigma to 4 sigma to 5 sigma will still reduce costs and increase customer satisfaction.

Sigma Level	Defects per Million	Yield
6	3.4	99.99966%
5	230	99.977%
4	6,210	99.38%
3	66,800	93.32%
2	308,000	69.15%
1	690,000	30.85%

Benefits of Six Sigma

Implementing Six Sigma within a business offers a number of benefits. However there are six key advantages that this methodology will offer any company.

1. *Improved Customer Loyalty*

Any business wants to retain its customers. Indeed, this is a significant factor in determining the success of a firm. But, of course, customer loyalty and retention only ever come as a result of high levels of customer satisfaction.

Surveys suggest the reasons given by most customers for not returning to a business are dissatisfaction with the experience and employee attitude. Often a company will not even know they have a dissatisfied customer as they will simply take their businesses elsewhere.

Implementing Six Sigma reduces the risk of your company having dissatisfied customers, for once training is complete, so few experiences should be outside of their specifications. To achieve this you may want to consider running a voice of the customer study which helps your business understand which of your products attributes are critical to the customer's perception of satisfaction.

2. *Time Management*

Employing a Six Sigma methodology at your business can help employees manage their time effectively, resulting in a more a efficient business and more productive employees. Users are asked to set SMART goals and then apply the data principles of Six Sigma to those goals. This is done by looking at three key areas; learning, performance and fulfilment.

For instance, under learning, a practitioner of Six Sigma might ask themselves; how often do interruptions take me away from my task and how many of these interruptions require my attention?

Similarly, under performance, they might consider how their practices are helping them reach their professional goals. Users can then create an action plan, the result of which can be employees who are up to 30 per cent more efficient and who are happier in themselves, having achieved a better work-life balance.

3. Reduced Cycle Time

Unfortunately, most projects firms embark on end up extending beyond their original deadline often because there are changes in project scope or there is a shift in management policy.

By using Six Sigma, a business can set up a team of experienced employees from all levels within the organisation and from every functional department. This team are then given the task of identifying factors that could negatively affect the project leading to long cycle times.

They can then be tasked to find solutions to these potential problems. This method allows business to create shorter cycle times for projects and stick to those schedules, with many firms reporting reductions in cycle times of up to 35 per cent.

4. Employee Motivation

Every business, if destined to succeed, needs its employees to act in the right way - but for employees to do so there must be sufficient motivation. Indeed, organisations who are willing to fully engage with employees have consistently demonstrated 25–50 per cent increases in productivity.

Sharing Six Sigma problem solving tools and techniques will allow for employee development and help create a climate and systems for employee motivation.

5. Strategic Planning

Six Sigma can play an integral part in any strategic vision. Once your business has used a created a mission statement and carried out a SWOT analysis, then Six Sigma can help you focus on areas for improvement.

For instance, if your business strategy is based on being a cost leader in the market, then Six Sigma can be used to improve internal processes, increase yields, eliminate unnecessary complexity and gain or maintain lowest cost supplier agreements. In fact, whatever your strategy happens to be, Six Sigma can help make your company the best at what it does.

6. *Supply Chain Management*

As previously mentioned, the aim of Six Sigma is to have a defect rate of less than 3.4 per million, and your suppliers have a major influence on whether this target is met. One of the possible ways to reduce the risk of defect is to use Six Sigma to drive down the number of suppliers your businesses has, as this in turn reduces the risk of defects.

It's also important to understand if your supplier is planning to implement any changes. For instance, a change in machinery can have an effect like the ripples from a rock thrown into a pond. The most successful firms drive their Six Sigma improvements as far up the supply chain as possible.

Global Strategy

Global strategy as defined in business terms is an organization's strategic guide to globalization. Such a connected world, allows a business's revenue to not be to be confined by borders. A business can employ a global business strategy to reap the rewards of trading in a worldwide market.

A global strategy involves thinking in an integrated way about all aspects of business-its suppliers, production sites, markets, and competition. It involves assessing every product or service from the perspective of both domestic and international market standards. It means embedding international perspectives in product formulations at the point of design, not as afterthoughts. It means meeting world standards even before seeking world markets and being world class even in local markets. It means deepening the company's understanding of local and cultural differences in order to become truly global.

The Key Drivers to globalization Driver

Global market Convergence

- Similar customer needs
- Global customers
- Transferable marketing Scale economies
- Global Issues Global Competition Government Influence Cost Advantages Global Strategies Trade policies
- Technical Standards
- host government
- policies Scale economies
- Sourcing efficiencies Countries costs

- High product development costs Interdependence
- Competitors global High export

Advantages & Disadvantages of International Operations

Advantages

1. Foreign operations can absorb excess production capacity, the benefits:
2. Allows firms to establish low –cost production facilities.
3. May be less competition
4. Reduce tariffs
5. Enables firms to learn technology and other cultures

Disadvantages

1. Firms confront with different cultures, sometime they cannot understand the rules of game
2. Dealing with different monetary systems can complicate international bus.

Global Challenge

1. How to gain and maintain exports to other international markets.
2. How to defend domestic markets against imported goods

Guidelines for Success as a Global Competitor Robert Allio Mentioned Guidelines for Customer Loyalty and Market Share

1. Get to know global markets first.
2. Counterattack at home for parent
3. Counterattack at home for parent firms (attack them at their homes).
4. Invest in new technology.
5. Consider alternative sources, e.g., establish in low labor cost
6. Install the right management at host countries.
7. Sacrifice short-term profit for longterm profit.
8. Join forces with competitors

Issues in Strategic Decision Making

A company would have different people in decision making at different periods of time. Decision often require judgments and thus is important to note that the person related factors are important in decision making and the decision make differ as that person changes. Â§ Again an individual does not take decisions alone. But often there is rumble in decisions, which could be between individual and group decision making. The decision taken by the group could be different from those that may be taken by the individual themselves. Â§ The company would need to decide on what criteria it should make its decision. Thus it need a process of objective setting, which serve as benchmarks for evaluation of the efficiency and effectiveness of the decision making process. There are three major criteria in decision making- the concept of maximization, - the concept of satisfying, -the concept of instrumentalism. Based on the chosen concept, Strategic decisions will differ. Â§ It is assumed that decision making is logical and thus there will be rationality in the decision making. In the context of Strategic decision making, it means that there would be a proper evaluation and then exercising a choice from among various alternative courses of action in such a way that it may lead to the achievement of the objectives in the best possible manner. As the situations are complex, straightforward thinking may not be effective. Creativity in decision making may be needed, thus the decision must be original and different. But also based on situation and circumstances there could be variability in decision making.

REFERENCES

Chapter I

- Read more: Strategic Management Definition Investopedia https://www.investopedia.com/terms/s/strategic-management.asp#ixzz53V68tkyQ Follow us: Investopedia on Facebook
- https://xisspm.files.wordpress.com/2010/09/strategic-management.pdf
- http://thebizmanagementguide.com/importance-of-strategic-management-in-business/
- https://bizfluent.com/list-7629680-four-basic-elements-strategic-management.html
    - Strategic Management: AbbassAlkhafaji and Richard Alan Nelson
    - Quick MBA: The Strategic Planning Process
- http://www.introduction-to-management.24xls.com/en215
- http://www.introduction-to-management.24xls.com/en213
- Strategic Management: Formulation and Implementation, RyszardBarnat, LLM., DBA, PhD (Strat. Mgmt)
- https://www.mbaskool.com/business-concepts/marketing-and-strategy-terms/7247-strategic-management-process.html
- http://www.balancedscorecard.org/BSC-Basics/Strategic-Planning-Basics
- http://www.simply-strategic-planning.com/benefits-of-strategic-planning.html
- https://2012books.lardbucket.org/books/marketing-principles-v1.0/s05-03-components-of-the-strategic-pl.html
- http://smallbusiness.chron.com/9-characteristics-effective-mission-statement-18142.html
- http://www.glennsmithcoaching.com/7-reasons-your-company-needs-clear-written-mission-statement/

Chapter II

- http://www.managementstudyguide.com/environmental-scanning.htm
- http://pestleanalysis.com/what-is-environmental-analysis/
- https://www.strategicmanagementinsight.com/tools/porters-five-forces.html
- www.strategicmanagementinsight.com
- mbajargons.com
- managementstudyguide.com
- managementinnovations.wordpress.com
- yourarticlelibrary.com
- iedunote.com
- smallbusiness.chron.com
- bizfluent.com
- citeman.com

- thepracticalleader.com
- www.keydifferences.com
- http://www.wisenepali.com
- http://www.yourarticlelibrary.com/organization/environmental-threat-and-opportunity-profile-%D0%B5%D1%82%D0%BE%D1%80/23557
- http://www.businessdictionary.com/definition/situation-analysis.html
- https://www.quora.com/Whats-the-difference-between-core-competency-and-competitive-advantage

Chapter III

- https://www.strategicmanagementinsight.com/tools/mckinsey-7s-model-framework.html
- https://www.mbaskool.com/business-concepts/marketing-and-strategy-terms/7505-strategic-gap-analysis.html
- https://www.clearpointstrategy.com/what-is-a-balanced-scorecard-definition/
- http://www.tools-and-techniques.24xls.com/en103

Chapter IV

- Peter F. Drucker. Management: Tasks, Responsibilities, Practices. New York: Harper & Row, 1974, pp. 498–504.

Chapter V

- http://www.untag-smd.ac.id/files/Perpustakaan_Digital_2/PUBLIC%20POLICY%20(Public%20administration%20and%20public%20policy%20102)%20Strategic%20Management%20for%20Public%20and%20N.pdf
- strategic management for public and non profit organization – Allen walter sties
- http://web.idv.nkmu.edu.tw/~hgyang/Module9.pdf
- http://www.bbamantra.com/strategic-evaluation-and-control/

Chapter VI

- http://www.answers.com/Q/State_the_global_issues_in_strategic_management
- http://www.referenceforbusiness.com/management/Str-Ti/Technology-Management.html
- http://www.bain.com/publications/articles/management-tools-business-process-reengineering.aspx
- https://www.isixsigma.com/methodology/total-quality-management-tqm/introduction-and-implementation-total-quality-management-tqm/
- http://asq.org/learn-about-quality/total-quality-management/overview/overview.html
- https://www.isixsigma.com/methodology/benchmarking/understanding-purpose-and-use-benchmarking/
- http://leansixsigmadefinition.com/glossary/six-sigma/

- https://www.processexcellencenetwork.com/lean-six-sigma-business-transformation/articles/6-ways-six-sigma-can-benefit-your-company
- https://www.cleverism.com/mergers-and-acquisitions-complete-guide/
- https://www.edupristine.com/blog/mergers-acquisitions
- https://www.tutorialspoint.com/strategic_management/diversification_strategies.htm

CHAPTER I

Brief Questions

1. Define strategic management.

Pg. 1

2. What are the various dimensions of strategic management?

Pg. 5

3. Write a short note on various levels of strategy.

Pg. 7

4. Differentiate strategy and tactics.

Pg. 9

Detail Questions

1. Explain the nature and importance of strategic management.

Pg. 1

2. Explain the elements of strategic management.

Pg. 4

3. Explain the strategic management process.

Pg. 6

4. What is mission? Explain its importance.

Pg. 11 & 13

5. Explain strategic planning process.

Pg. 10

CHAPTER II

Brief Questions

1. Write a short note on environmental scanning.

Pg. 20

2. Write a brief note on value chain analysis.

Pg. 33

3. Differentiate cost advantage and differentiation advantage.

Pg. 36

Detail Questions

1. Explain PEST.

Pg. 22

2. Explain Porter's five forces model.

Pg. 25

3. Explain using the Porter's five forces model.

Pg. 27

4. Explain SWOT Analysis.

Pg. 29

5. Explain ETOP with an example.

Pg. 32

<h1 style="text-align:center">CHAPTER III</h1>

Brief Questions

1. Define strategic choice.

Pg. 39

2. Brief out the various steps in implementing Mc Kinsey 7s model.

Pg. 41

3. What is strategic Gap analysis?

Pg. 45

4. What are the pros and cons of GE Nine cell matrix?

Pg. 46

5. Differentiate GE McKinsey and BCG matrices.

Pg. 48

6. List the uses of balanced score card.

Pg. 52

Detail Questions

1. Describe BCG matrix with its limitations.

Pg. 39

2. Mc Kinsey 7 s-Elucidate.

Pg. 41

3. How will you analyse from the nine cells of the GE Matrix?

Pg. 46

4. Analyse the various stages of life of product.

Pg. 52

CHAPTER IV

Brief Questions

1. How will you implement a strategy?

Pg. 54

2. Write a brief outline about barriers in strategic implementation.

Pg. 56

3. Why strategic implementation is important?

Pg. 57

4. What are the functions of top level management?

Pg. 62

5. Brief about resource allocation and list the factors that affects resource allocation.

Pg. 66

6. What is strategic control and its specifications?

Pg. 69

Detail Questions

1. How will a strategic plan fail? Explain.

Pg. 54

2. Characteristics of Strategic Decisions-Explain in detail.

Pg. 58

3. Explain the Process of Strategy Implementation.

Pg. 60

4. CEO-Elucidate his role.

Pg. 63

5. How will a resource be allocated?

Pg. 67

CHAPTER V

Brief Questions

1. Define strategic control and state its importance.

Pg. 71

2. What are the criteria for a successful business?

Pg. 72

3. Differentiate strategic and operational control.

Pg. 78

4. What are the various categories of evaluation?

Pg. 88

5. What are the criteria for evaluation?

Pg. 89

Detail Questions

1. Explain the barriers in strategic evaluation and control

Pg. 79

2. Explain the control process in detail.

Pg. 82

3. Describe about qualitative and quantitative factors.

Pg. 85

4. Explain the process of strategic evaluation.

Pg. 87

CHAPTER VI

Brief Questions

1. How will you manage technology and innovation?

Pg. 90

2. Write about the types of mergers and acquisitions.

Pg. 93

3. Why does an M & A fail?

Pg. 95

4. What is diversification? State its types.

Pg. 96

5. What is BPR? What are the steps involved in it?

Pg. 98

6. Differentiate benchmarking and competitor research.

Pg. 103

Detail Questions

1. Mergers and acquisitions-Write about the considerations to be made and the various stages in it.

Pg. 93

2. Explain the principles of TQM.

Pg. 100

3. Explain the steps involved in benchmarking.

Pg. 104

4. Brief about six sigma and explain its benefits.

Pg. 106

5. Write a detailed note on global strategy.

Pg. 109